PENGUIN BOOKS
LAURIE BAKER: LIFE, WORK, WRITINGS

Born in 1952, Gautam Bhatia graduated in fine arts and did his post-graduate studies in architecture at the University of Pennsylvania. Bhatia is the recipient of several national and international awards for his architectural work and study.

He is the author of *Punjabi Baroque and Other Memories of Architecture*; *Silent Spaces and Stories of Architecture*; *Malaria Dreams and Other Visions of Architecture*; *Punchtantra: Parables for the 21st Century*; *A Short History of Everything* and editor of *Eternal Stone: Great Buildings of India*.

Gautam Bhatia lives and practises in New Delhi.

By the same author

Punjabi Baroque and Other Memories of Architecture
Silent Spaces and Other Stories of Architecture
Malaria Dreams and Other Visions of Architecture
Punchtantra: Parables for the 21ˢᵗ Century
A Short History of Everything
Eternal Stone: Great Buildings of India (Ed.)

Gautam Bhatia

LAURIE BAKER
Life, Work, Writings

PENGUIN BOOKS

Penguin Books India (P) Ltd., 11 Community Centre, Panchsheel Park, New Delhi 110017, India
Penguin Books Ltd., 27 Wrights Lane, London W8 5TZ, UK
Penguin Putnam Inc., 375 Hudson Street, New York, NY 10014, USA
Penguin Books Australia Ltd., Ringwood, Victoria, Australia
Penguin Books Canada Ltd., 10 Alcorn Avenue, Suite 300, Toronto, Ontario MAV 3B2, Canada
Penguin Books (NZ) Ltd., Cnr Rosedale & Airborne Roads, Albany, Auckland, New Zealand

First published in Viking by Penguin Books India 1991
Published in Penguin Books 1994

The author and the publishers would like to thank Ram Rehman and Jack Skeel for granting permission to use their pictures on pages 26, 127 and 160 respectively, and V.S. Rawat for the architectural drawings.

This project was sponsored by HUDCO.

Contents

vi

Acknowledgements

I am grateful to Mr S.K. Sharma and Mr M.N. Joglekar of HUDCO for having funded this project. The amount of time Laurie Baker spent with me—talking about his work, correcting my notes and interpretations, explaining, even writing—may have been better spent in building ten other houses. Monisha Mukundan's meticulous editing in the early stages, and Damini Singh's rewriting and ideas on sequence helped to shape a rough, often unwieldy, text.

I would also like to express my gratitude to the editors of *World Architecture*, *Spazio Societa*, *Architectural Review*, *Inside Outside*, *Indian Express* and *Times of India* for allowing me to extract quotations from their publications.

Without Gayatri Ratnam many of Baker's houses would have remained undocumented, as some of them indeed have. Thanks also to Navin Gupta, Jayshree Nair, V.S. Rawat, and others in the office, who were always ready with suggestions on design and layout. I would also like to thank Mr and Mrs T.C. Alexander. Living in a Laurie Baker house, they infected me with their own brand of enthusiasm and generously shared their home with me, providing new insights to a little-known city.

My sincere gratitude to David Polk in Philadelphia and Anant Raje in Ahmedabad. Though theirs is not a measurable contribution to the book, it is the many years that I have known them as thoughtful practitioners of the profession and as teachers and friends that have shaped my perceptions of building, the way that I see architecture.

No wife ever goes without due acknowledgement in a husband's first book. Ritu gave little by way of wifely encouragement, and she did not prepare endless cups of coffee to keep me awake. But she did do her share. Her greatest asset was the offering of an unbridled and innocent appreciation of Laurie Baker's architecture. For this I am grateful.

Foreword

I first met Laurie Baker in the early 1980s in Madhya Pradesh, but it was only after I joined HUDCO as Chairman and Managing Director in 1985 that I had the opportunity of seeing his buildings in Kerala. It was then that I realized that his was a master's hand. Baker's locally active methods and simple innovations had created economical and attractive forms for all: whether poor or rich, a school or a church, the specifications, textures and architectural manners were always similar. This commonality of approach, he reasoned, was essential to create any impact on housing in a country the size of India.

Laurie Baker is truly the Hassan Fathy of India. People say that Baker has developed his architecture based on the vernacular architecture of Kerala, respecting the local climate—the hot and humid climate of the region—and environment while designing his buildings. While this is certainly true, I might add that his architecture also has a universal applicability.

Laurie Baker's message is loud and clear—economize on materials and provide quality homes through better-trained and better-organized artisans. This message has legitimacy not only for the building activity in India but also for other developing countries.

And yet, just as the purity of the traditional *ragas* has to be maintained through constant practice, Laurie Baker's ideas should be maintained through sustained application. Today, Baker's designs and ideas have brought about a movement. A number of young architects, from Kerala and other parts of India are spreading his architectural approach to all parts of the country. They build homes which look, are, and cost 'Laurie Baker'. HUDCO too is promoting Baker's ideas and technology through training programmes. Concepts on mud construction are being promoted through HUDCO's Laurie Baker Mud Foundation.

HUDCO's sponsorship of this book is seen in the light of bringing to the public eye, these and other ideas on thoughtful low-cost design; but more than that, the book is meant as a kind of practical tribute to a gifted and generous architect.

New Delhi   *S.K. Sharma*
June 1991

Author's Note

Some years ago, an employee of the Organization for Urban Housing recounted to me how an invitation to a national seminar on housing had been turned down by Laurie Baker. The meeting was meant to discuss the allocation of billions of rupees for housing and to take a decision on the policy towards the twenty million houses that were required in the country in the next five-year plan. It was an important meeting of a core group headed by the prime minister; the ten days of discussion were to produce a paper that would improve the lot of the country's homeless. But Laurie Baker refused to attend the seminar and in a letter thanking the prime minister for the invitation he stated his views on the subject of housing. Inside the envelope was also a statement of the expenses that they would have incurred had he accepted the invitation. Airfare for a trip to Trivandrum, taxi fare, hotel accommodation and meals for ten days, plus a daily stipend—all of which added up to over Rs 30,000. According to Baker the money would have been better spent in actually providing housing to two needy families he knew locally in Trivandrum; their names, addresses and details of destitution were also enclosed in the letter along with the request that these funds be despatched quickly to them so that construction could begin before the monsoons hit Kerala.

I am fortunate to have experienced something of the integrity of Baker's life in the few years I spent recording his work in the late eighties. The book was originally intended to be a guide to his method of building, but over the many meetings in the veranda of his home, the Hamlet, and the numerous visits to the sites (occasionally carrying a client's door on the roof of his car) and watching him communicate with the Malyalee masons with vigorous gestures, I came to realize that Baker's architecture is a by-product of a larger picture—a picture that recognizes the importance of people's aspirations for a better life. I began to see that his buildings were merely a direct and honest response to this spirit, this idea. It was after having realized this that the book took a different turn.

Baker's past, his religious affiliation, his experience and lifestyle, assumed an importance beyond the normal scope of the study of an architectural career. It is these that gave the book its form—*Laurie Baker:*

Life, Work, Writings contains the three inseparable facets of a single man, each influencing and affecting the other.

In the ten years since the first edition of the book Baker has gone on to build several new institutions in Kerala and gift his precious time to projects in earthquake and cyclone-affected areas. Despite his advancing years, he continues to work with a passion that hasn't dimmed. Baker's originality has meant going back to origins—to an understanding of a common and comprehensive way of living.

The directness and simplicity of Laurie Baker's own work made it essential that the book be intended for all: the interested lay reader, the architect, and the student of architecture—anyone with even a passing interest in ideas of design, low cost building, or the life of a committed individual. But while a public readership calls for a general text—an 'atmosphere' created of words and photographs—the professional and the practitioner seek the technicalities of plan and details. Though on the outset the resolution of this duality appeared difficult, the text was kept entirely presentational, free of polemics or controversies on Third World housing. I was purely a chronicler, an interpreter of the man and his ideas. It is in this spirit that I hope the book will be received.

New Delhi   *Gautam Bhatia*
January 2000

Section I

LIFE

Baker's Contribution to Architecture

I learn my architecture by watching what ordinary people do; in any case it is always the cheapest and simplest because ordinary people do it. They don't even employ builders, the families do it themselves. The job works, you can see it in the old buildings—the way wood lattice work with a lot of little holes filters the light and glare. I'm absolutely certain that concrete frames filled with glass panels is not the answer.

My clients have always been Indian. I've not even had the foreign-returned to deal with, since I work primarily with the poor and I've always wanted to give people what they want and what they need which obviously is all Indian. My feeling as an architect is that you're not after all trying to put up a monument which will be remembered as a 'Laurie Baker Building' but Mohan Singh's house where he can live happily with his family.[1]

Laurie Baker has worked in India for over forty years now. He is one of the very few architects who has had the opportunity and the stamina to work on such a remarkably varied spectrum of projects ranging from fishermen's villages to institutional complexes and from low-cost mud-housing schemes to low-cost cathedrals. In Trivandrum alone he has built over a thousand houses. Besides this, his work includes forty churches, numerous schools, institutions and hospitals.

It is not only the number of buildings that Laurie Baker has designed and the range of architectural commissions he has executed that sets him apart from other architects. What makes his work even more remarkable is the way in which he draws creative sustenance from the environment in which he works, absorbing vernacular patterns of construction and individual styles of living to such a degree that he is able to give his clients the comfort and ease of homes and institutions that are firmly rooted in the soil upon which they stand. All this is done keeping in mind the special needs of those who will inhabit or use these places.

In the designing of these varied projects, Laurie Baker takes half-forgotten vernacular patterns of design and construction from the rural

3

setting to dislocated urban residents whose building choices are often limited to the unsuitable structural concepts discarded in the West. In every building that Baker designs, he asserts the appropriateness of traditional construction to local conditions, adapting existing locally-available materials and traditional methods to contemporary urban structures.

A recognition of Baker's contribution to architecture has a singular timeliness today. It has come at a time when a questing conscience has provoked the developing world—concerned with growth that is appropriate—to look inwards, to solutions of its own making. In these circumstances, Baker in India remains a lone protagonist, experimenting singly and quietly in a distant corner of the country and providing information on the causes and results of his numerous architectural interventions.

In both, his work and writings, Baker emphatically rejects the 'international style' that lingers so perniciously in India. The French architect,

Le Corbusier, who designed Chandigarh, spawned a host of acolytes seeking a universally applicable architectural technology. The result of this is seen in the post- fifties buildings of almost every city in India. Baker has never accepted the idea that the multiplicity of human needs and aspirations can be fulfilled by a standard set of design options and materials. He believes that individual needs stem from India's diverse environment, the varying cultural patterns and lifestyles; and he feels that these needs must be met through an architecture which is responsive, uses local materials and expresses itself in many different forms.

In Baker's scheme of things, architecture cannot be transplanted without doing violence to those very needs which it is attempting to meet. When, for example, the introverted patterns of desert architecture are transferred to the fertile landscapes of the Kerala coast, it dislocates traditional patterns of living. Parallels to this may be seen in any mass-housing scheme, when all-too-often, inhabitants are compelled to camp uncomfortably within unsuitable contours and divisions of space.

However, Baker is no conservative. He is at pains to emphasize the fact that living architecture thrives on appropriate assimilation and adaptation. Indeed, its vitality frequently stems from its ability to change and to meet the changing needs and perceptions of its inhabitants. Architecture, like any craft, is an organic, evolving form; and traditional patterns are not the rigidly-structured creations of individuals but the collective experience of many generations. Baker's architecture draws inspiration from the work of successive generations of builders, from the imprint of the environment and those who have lived in it. In his case it happens to be his adopted home state of Kerala in south India.

The building techniques Baker has evolved to suit specific problems of his poorer clients in Kerala is not a formula applicable to all similar situations; and yet, from it stems an entire ideology of architectural practice—a pattern that is revolutionary in its simplicity and its contradiction of the accepted norms of architecture in contemporary India. Baker's work is an effective demonstration of his own strength, his own interpretation of tradition, technology and lifestyle.

Influences

Distinctive architectural styles were not designed by some famous ancient architect who decreed that a certain style will be used in Japan and a certain other style will be used in Peru and yet another style in Punjab. The upturned, horned roofs of buildings as found in Kerala, China and Japan are the direct result of the people of those places making use of the most common, plentiful, useful material: bamboo—to house and protect them from natural enemies such as sun, rain, hurricanes and wind. A completely different set of styles has evolved in hot, dry, treeless, desert areas, as in parts of Egypt, Iran and India; in almost every district in the world these natural styles have grown to the patterns that could be seen in the first half of this century.

Our 'backward' ancestors had learned how to live with and cope with the problems of climate. They had learned that a pitched or a sloping roof lessened the effects of all these hazards. They knew the movements of air currents and placed their wall openings almost at ground level. They knew that hot air rises and allowed it to travel upwards from the low eaves to the openings at the ends of the high ridge. They understood and applied principles of insulation; their roofing materials formed hollow cellular protective layers and their storage spaces provided insulation from the midday sun. They had understood that wall surfaces can absorb and retain just as much heat as a roof surface, so they kept these walls as small in area as possible and never left them unprotected. They knew that eye-strain from working out in the sun could be alleviated by rest in an area where glare was eliminated and they used smooth, hard, light-coloured surfaces sparingly and left the natural materials—wood, laterite, brick, stone—exposed. Their practical knowledge of the properties of these differing building materials was amazing. They knew, for instance, how to design their timber and wood work to avoid warping, twisting and cracking.[2]

Laurie Baker's philosophy of architecture is inextricably bound with his experiences of childhood and youth in England, and, later, in the Pithoragarh district of Uttar Pradesh in the Himalayas where he lived for sixteen years.

One of his earliest architecture-related memories is that of being baffled by the differences in the styles of houses at the seaside, where he went on holidays, and that of houses in the mountains, where he lived.

When he was seventeen, he went on a cycling tour of Europe with friends. He was fascinated by the unfolding vistas of nature, landscapes, cities and people. The differences in the life-patterns of the people and the differences in the houses from country to country left an indelible impression on his mind.

By the time he returned from the tour he was already thinking of a career in architecture, and, soon afterwards, enrolled at the Birmingham School of Architecture. He graduated in 1937. However, the Second World War broke out before he could complete the period of professional apprenticeship. During the war Baker enlisted in the Friends Ambulance Unit and was sent to China as part of a surgical unit serving in the war between China and Japan. He then went to Burma and, in the midst of bitter fighting, was involved in tending to severely-wounded victims. His unit thus learnt to function under the most difficult circumstances. Later, Baker worked with the civilian population, dealing with people suffering from leprosy. He became deeply involved with the work he was doing, but the hardships he had endured took their toll on

the treatment 'throne' in the hospital

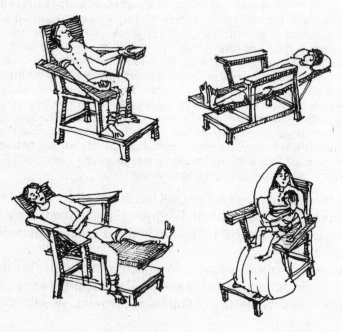

his health and he was sent back to England to recuperate. On his way back, while waiting for a ship at Bombay, he had a chance encounter with Mahatma Gandhi whose philosophy was to be a major influence in his work.

When in England, Baker heard of a worldwide organization dealing with leprosy in India. As he explains it, 'The organization wanted a builder–architect–engineer sort of person, with planning and building experience and with a knowledge of leprosy and its treatment, to convert old refugee centres into actual treatment hospitals. So it was to this job that I came back to India in 1945.'

Newer kinds of treatments and cures for leprosy were being developed at the time. The mission for which Baker worked already had ninety refugee and leprosy homes in India, all of which were in remote areas. The buildings in which they were housed were becoming increasingly inadequate for the new forms of treatments. Baker's job often included renovating old buildings and transforming old asylums into modern hospitals with the smallest possible expenditure. He worked and lived in various parts of the country gaining valuable knowledge of a variety of simple building styles and experience in dealing with all kinds of materials. 'I preferred to live with an Indian and his family,' he says, speaking of this period in his life, 'At one of these leprosy hospitals in the state of Uttar Pradesh, I stayed with a family called Chandy. My host's sister, Elizabeth Jacob, was a doctor working in a hospital in Hyderabad. We met and decided to get married... There was the obvious and natural opposition from various friends and family members to such a mixed marriage.'

The couple decided to wait. Elizabeth carried on with her work in the same mission in Hyderabad, and Baker continued to travel from one leprosy hospital to another—carrying out architectural improvements, and in some cases building anew to accommodate the equipment and the new systems of treatment that were being introduced by the mission doctors. He and Elizabeth would see each other whenever their work permitted. They found that they were beginning to disagree with some of the mission's ideologies. But they continued to work devotedly for the cause to which both were, by now, firmly committed. However, their dissatisfaction with the mission grew and, eventually, they left their jobs in 1948. They were married soon afterwards.

While on a trekking honeymoon at the foothills of Kumaon the Bakers decided to settle down in Pithoragarh in the Himalayas. Baker recalls, 'After walking and climbing miles from anywhere we stopped to rest and recover and relax in a place a few miles above Pithoragarh. Immediately, people having no access to medical facilities discovered Kuni (Elizabeth) was a doctor. They gave us accommodation and immediately we were in business and set up our first little hospital in a disused tea shop.'

Baker's view of Pithoragarh

The Bakers remained in Pithoragarh for the next sixteen years. It was here, while living amongst the poor in the most adverse climatic conditions and in uncompromising hill terrain, that Laurie Baker came to understand the value of vernacular building.

I am these days sometimes quoted as an expert or an authority on
'appropriate' or 'intermediate' technology and although I did not know it at
the time, it was my life and experiences at Pithoragarh that taught me
'appropriate and intermediate' technology. . . .

To me, this Himalayan domestic architecture was a perfect example of
vernacular architecture. Simple, efficient, inexpensive. . . .As usual this
delightful, dignified housing demonstrated hundreds of years of building
research on how to cope with local materials, how to cope with local climate
hazards and how to accommodate the local social pattern of living. It dealt
with incidental difficult problems of how to build on a steeply sloping site,
or how to cope with earthquakes and how to avoid landsliding areas and
paths. The few examples of attempts to modernize housing merely

house and home

11

demonstrated, only too clearly, our modern conceit and showed how very foolish we are when we attempt to ignore or abandon these hundreds of years of 'research' in local building materials. . . .[3]

Memories of Mountain Living

making bread in a cooking pot

the two types of angeethi

The direct and honest use of local materials created its own expression of structural necessity, of economic restraint. Confronted with building materials like rock, mud, laterite and cow-dung, Baker's architectural practice in the Himalayas was anything but conventional. His education at the Birmingham School of Architecture and the skills acquired during his professional apprenticeship in England became decidedly insignificant in the austere mountain environment in which he found himself. He realized that the local people knew how to use materials more effectively than he did.

the washing machine (ritha was added to this)

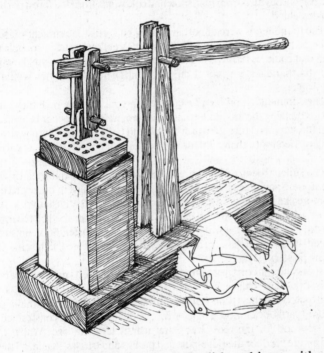

It was a very unusual sight to see an English architect, with an urban background, working with and learning from mountain tribesmen and village masons, and using indigenous materials for building. However, it proved to be a richly fruitful alliance. Baker learnt to adapt his skills and training to the needs with which he was now faced. He built schools, hospitals and community buildings, all of which ran on a self-supporting basis. The structures produced were naturally low key and instinctive—by-products of the site conditions and the local skills available. And yet, they were the beginning of what was to develop into the unique Baker style of architecture.

Village planning and site utilization were equally functional and delightfully simple. Usually there were rows (terraces) of houses all joined together with common dividing partition walls; sometimes when anywhere from three to ten or twelve brothers lived in such a row of houses, the front veranda was common to all. These multi-housed rows of dwellings were usually under one big long common roof. The row followed the contours wherever possible, and as a consequence was sometimes curved. The row of houses was usually sited to overlook the terraced fields below, to catch the sunshine, and to get protection from rain, snow and cold winds from the forest or steep hillside behind.

The foundations were almost invariably built on stone straight off solid rock—a foundation of Mother Earth herself. Very rarely did the people use earth that could be terraced or cultivated, but they chose their building sites along rocks, ridges or spurs of the mountains where cultivation would be impossible.

Their foundation problems were therefore nil, and the rock they quarried for building the foundation and basement walls was split or blasted out from the same bed rock on which they would build. I never saw any rubble being carried more than a hundred yards and, of course, it was all carried on someone's head.

The superstructure walls were also built of the same quarried-on-the-spot stone. Sometimes it was big and square and chunky, in other places it was more like thick slate in large sheets or slabs only a few inches thick. And of course it was all built in mud mortar. The walls were heaped on the inside with mud, or mud and cow-dung, or lime mortar or plaster. Sometimes the outside was left as it was, or, sometimes, it too was treated with some sort of lime plaster.

Doors and windows were often of delightfully shaped and simply carved woodwork using chir-pine or deodar, or occasionally some other local country wood such as tuni. But this timber was always found within a few hundred yards, or at most a mile or two, of the house being constructed.

The wood for the roofs was extravagantly lavish in size. Whole tree trunks were used for the ridge-pole and purlins and trusses. Again, all these roofing materials were close at hand. Occasionally a wealthier person would send a few miles for a thinner quality of slate which could be shaped and squared, but this was their form of showing off and was not a necessity and fortunately not often indulged in. This whole roof construction over the wall construction, was completely adequate to cope with the climatic extremes of heat and dryness in summer, with the violent rain storms, and with the heavy snow in the winter.[4]

14

The strength and the organic resilience of Baker's early architecture was the direct outcome of his own strength and resilience. And, in turn, the years of continuous settlement in a single place gave his designs a quality of rootedness. The lessons he derived from this experience in the Himalayas and the architectural principles he learnt there remained with him even when, years later, he resumed practice in Trivandrum.

The Bakers left Pithoragarh in 1963 and moved to a similar hill area in central Kerala. They settled in a remote village, Vakamon, inhabited by tribal people and Tamil migrants, and continued to work in much the same way as they had in Pithoragarh—building schools and leprosy treatment centres, using their skills and training for the benefit of the local people, and learning local skills as they did so.

Several years later, while on a holiday at Trivandrum, they got involved with leprosy work in the southern city and just stayed on.

In Trivandrum, Baker applied all that he had learnt to a wider clientele—building homes for the middle class and institutions for a wide range of organizations. Today, over a thousand families in the Trivandrum district live in Baker's houses; and the evolution of his style can be traced through his work in and around this city.

As he worked, Baker began to understand the essential simplicity that is at the base of effective, living architecture. He refined his style, stepping away from unnecessary accoutrements. A chance encounter with Mahatma Gandhi at the beginning of his career seems to have made a great impact on his architecture, as Gandhi's ideologies were to influence him in all his work. Though this is not the single most persuasive influence in Baker's life, in the course of several discourses of the Mahatma, Baker imbibed the meaning of one of his most persistent messages—that change in post-independent India can be brought about only through education and revival of the local crafts and cottage industries; that is, real independence can be only achieved by self-reliance and by encouraging local craftsmanship. Unfortunately, much too often this message has been lost in the muddy waters of politics and the race to modernize India. Thus Baker's work is more relevant particularly now than ever before.

I believe that Gandhiji is the only leader in our country who has talked consistently with common-sense about the building needs of our country. What he said many years ago is even more pertinent now. One of the things he said that impressed me and has influenced my thinking more than anything else was that the ideal houses in the ideal village will be built of materials which are all found within a five-mile radius of the house. What clearer explanation is there of what appropriate building technology means than this advice by Gandhiji. I confess that as a young architect, born, brought up, educated and qualified in the West, I thought at first Gandhiji's ideal was a bit 'far-fetched' and I used to argue to myself that of course he probably did not intend us to take this ideal too literally.

But now, in my seventies and with forty years of building behind me, I have come to the conclusion that he was right, literally word for word, and that he did not mean that there could be exceptions. If only I had not been so proud and sure of my learning and my training as an architect, I could have seen clearly wonderful examples of Gandhiji's wisdom all round me throughout the entire period I lived in the Pithoragarh district.[5]

Baker's instinctive response to Gandhi's simplicity and his acceptance of the frugal style of life in Pithoragarh stems perhaps from his Quaker background. The rigorous Quaker upbringing, with its emphasis on simplicity and austerity, its rejection of all ornament and luxury as sinful self-indulgence, was reinforced by the theories of modernism that were current during his architectural training—the one complementing the other. And so, though Baker's work appears to emanate from the functional doctrines of the modern movement, it is largely the outcome of his Quaker past. If the modernist ideology dictated that design be determined by purpose and by the mechanical process by which it is realized, the Quakers arrived at a similar conclusion from a different starting point. The sort of burdened and forced functionalism that the modern doctrine enforced with elaborate theory, came naturally to those whose religious beliefs sought to express in their handiwork the desire to labour willingly and honestly.

Quaker craftsmanship has become a byword for harmonious proportions, finely-executed workmanship and simple elegance. These qualities emanate from a deeply-held belief that each piece of work is an offering to God and must, therefore, not only be without flaw, but must not violate God's creation in the making. From this stems a natural inclination to use the materials cautiously, leading to a conservationist approach to design. Baker's deep convictions and the persistent inten-

16

tion to eliminate ornamentation is achieved in forms that are themselves so pure, so free of self-consciousness, that their beauty lies only in their soundness of construction and the perfection of craftsmanship.

Baker's architecture, firmly anchored to his Quaker beliefs, is ordered by the considerations and circumstances of this ancient ecclesiastical consciousness. To enter a room, a hall, a house built by him is to become immediately aware of this profound connection. For, in this rugged countenance of rubble masonry, in the quiet of whitewashed brick, amongst low built-in furnishings and the subdued light of latticed walls, is evidence of a deep tranquility of mind, a single realization that the origin of the space comes from more than just economic and structural conditions.

Baker's personal accord with a way of life and a way of work invests his buildings with the values he cherishes. In designing objects finely constructed and complete in themselves, there is a reflection of Baker's intensely realized faith, his unusual set of principles imbibed from the laws and customs of his religious sect. This attitude to life and work is so deeply rooted in this distinct philosophy that it has established—even amongst people of different faiths—a unique architectural tradition.

The large body of work that now exists makes it possible to understand the consistency of quality, craft and design that has spanned Baker's forty-five-year-old career. It is easy, perhaps, to draw conclusions about a number of striking influences from this vantage point. In fact it matters little whether one set of influences is greater or more pervasive than the other—whether the encounter with Mahatma Gandhi or the projects at the leprosy centres during the Second World War influenced his work in later life or whether his upbringing as a Quaker set the tone for his professional practice. The 'rightness' of Baker's architecture and the harmonious balance between his life and work comes from the way his spirit percolates all his activities. But there is little doubt that the cumulative effect of an unconventional background and experience can be best judged by those who have known Laurie Baker—known him as an architect and lived in his buildings.

Context

There is a general belief that India is wealthy, both in simple basic building materials and in potential labour forces. Then there is a firm unyielding belief that all this talk of 'low-cost building' should not be 'for the poor' but for *all*. Furthermore, although we possess a certain amount of more sophisticated building materials, such supplies are comparatively small and must be used to maximum advantage. For example, we possess steel but the fact remains that many mechanical industries have a stronger claim on its use than the building industry, which can, if it wants, find substitutes and alternatives.[6]

At the turn of the century, architects genuinely believed that the modern movement would provide new techniques and new materials to serve the needs of ordinary people. It seemed as if technology could provide a solution to the persistent problem of housing, and it was believed that high-tech buildings would ultimately improve the standard of living for everybody.

However, rapid industrialization only seemed to increase the demand for housing that has now grown to unimaginable proportions. Housing has come to be dominated almost entirely by commercial builders employed by local governments—both of whom look upon a house as a commodity to be produced and sold in large numbers. The once-new technological solutions of the modern movement have fossilized into rigid inflexibility in their hands. The comfort and lifestyle of the individuals for whom the mass-housing schemes are intended are very rarely considered. The result is all-too-visible in cities all over the world. Especially, in Third World countries such as India, as governments struggle to house the ever-increasing numbers of urban dwellers, the inadequacies of the forty-year-old doctrines of modern architecture have been brought more sharply into focus. Moreover, as the gap between available resources and the need for housing has increased, the inflexible sterility of the modern movement has become even more apparent.

Mass-housing and emphasis on the improvement of living conditions is all a result of the new industrial economy. Humanistic considerations are no longer the primary logic for the evaluation of design. This has led to a break from tradition and given us an increasing number of impersonal, anonymous buildings. Unfamiliarity with this new kind of architecture adversely affects the psyche of the people inhabiting it.

> The necessity for speed was one of the big factors that contributes to that break with tradition. It probably took a thousand years for us to find out by trial-and-error how to make a mud wall impervious to rain and wind, another thousand years to learn how to keep termites out of it, and another two or three thousand to learn how to build multi-storeyed mud buildings.[7]

Though Baker is not a founder, practitioner or product of the modern doctrine in any sense, he has, in own career, demonstrated similar concerns. But, unlike the movement, in his endeavour to improve living conditions architecturally he seeks a purposeful link with tradition.

Baker's work can be viewed as part of a much larger worldwide effort to re-examine architectural values. In the 1960s, the new architect's rejection of establishment values was an admission that the profession was out of touch with the times. Ordinary human needs to which the modern doctrine was as wholeheartedly committed seemed imprisoned in unfamiliar buildings and surroundings. The increasing inability of government agencies to produce adequate housing led architects in several parts of the developing world to examine architectural priorities. The work of John Turner in Latin America and Hassan Fathy's experience in Egypt paralleled the quiet revolution that Laurie Baker was enacting in India.

Each one sought the development of a contemporary vernacular—a commonly observed, felt and accepted language of building which would be transformed to suit the new requirements. The prevalence of an overriding craft tradition and the need to evolve buildings out of severe economic constraints shifted the emphasis away from technology towards an earthy humanism. Such a transformation required a sharp comprehension of the dual phenomena of tradition and change; and of the need to re-establish the use of traditional construction without the

19

actual imitation of traditional styles. The new vocabulary is one to which Baker's architecture can readily address while also taking the optimum benefits from the new building materials.

Concrete, a major building material of the modern movement, was

meant to span greater areas; but Baker uses its qualities of rugged lightness, in combination with those of the traditional terracotta tile roof, to produce a contemporary version of the vernacular. Similarly, laterite and brick walls reduced to the minimum envelope required for enclosure are not, in themselves, an innovation, but his use of these materials strikes an unusual compromise between traditional practice and modern principle—thus deftly illustrating how contemporary requirements of the house can easily be met by such an adaptation.

In every respect, Baker's work is in startling contrast to architectural practice in practically every part of the country. Years of colonial rule and the architecture of Corbusier has effectively ensured that buildings of post-independent India have little basis in the architecture of the past. Today, the desire for modernity has provoked the Indian client and the architect into fantasies that have little or no connection to the locale and the prevailing conditions. Buildings are produced without corporate, regional or historic identity. It is from this climate of aesthetic uncertainty that architects have sought relief in decoration and pop-iconography. Their recent works have drawn heavily—in a decorative

21

and interpretive way—upon the history of style, rather than the history of architecture. The stylized pediment, the bloated keystone, and fake capitals and columns have become the most visible links to the past. The association with tradition now has little to do with the nature of space, plan and habitation, and has been reduced to the cartoon quality of an advertising bill-board.

Such an architecture has arisen from motives that are intentional and self-conscious. Its detachment from place, people and context has produced a kind of building that is no longer the frame, the backdrop for society. The concern for climate, location, vegetation and living pattern has been ignored as architecture is parcelled along political and market boundaries. Consequently, the modern architect can no longer comprehend the complex nature of rootedness. His obsession with these signs and symbols seems nothing more than the continual desire to communicate to his peers and to maintain architecture as a mainstream profession among the public. He has become incapable of suggesting anything more than just his immediate construction—isolated and often in conflict with the environment in which it is placed. In these conditions an imaginative assessment of the relation between the client and society seems almost impossible.

Baker looks upon the imitation of foreign techniques of building and the superficial superimposition of Indian details as aspects that only exaggerate the poverty of the country's architecture. He seeks to convey the conditions of a place through the medium of building; the medium may be the material, the design or the technique of construction, but in so doing every project also makes a larger statement of the society in which it is set.

By AD 2000, the Indian population will, it is estimated, be one billion. If the present trend continues there will be a demand for fifty million new houses, almost half of what exist in the country today, along with a proportionate requirement for facilities—schools, markets, institutions, and public amenities. With the increased demand for building, architecture will necessarily have to make broader, more socially-conscious strokes. A re-examination of technology and lifestyles is an obvious and imperative outcome of the challenges facing a country of one billion.

22

But our modern, advanced scientific minds should know how to assess the merits and demerits of historical and factual evidence of the way people who have lived in a particular setting and climate, have coped with the problems which are still inevitably ours today. To brush aside all this demonstration and evidence as old-fashioned and therefore useless, is extremely foolish. Having made our assessment we would show ourselves capable of adopting the lessons we have learned (negative or positive, they are of equal importance) to our current living habits and the currently available building materials at our disposal. Along with this we should remind ourselves that it is not 'Advancement' or 'Development' or 'Progress' to indulge in modern building materials and techniques at tremendous expenses and to no good effect when there is no justification or reason for their use, instead of older, simpler, inexpensive methods.[8]

In every society there will always be extravagant buildings commissioned by the rich, there will always be commercial and political complexes and public sector undertakings; but compared to the rest of the building requirements these are miniscule endeavours. Unless architecture transcends its traditional scope, architects will do incalculable damage to the environment and to the existing patterns of a traditional society. That, Baker maintains, is precisely the crisis of architecture in

India. In a country beset with such pressing problems and challenges, architecture remains a profession of the elite.

Modern architecture in India has continuously stressed individual building; books and design journals continue to publish only the work of individual genius. In the face of the pressing needs of designing for an ever-increasing population with constantly expanding aspirations, the creation of isolated masterpieces by acknowledged artists becomes nothing more than an over-indulgence. There has never been an attempt to define in simple terms the kind of setting Indians would like to live in—an architecture that identifies with an Indian sense of place. It is this identification with place, which becomes apparent in Baker's own commitment to the housing needs of the common man.

The Craftsman's Legacy

In the building world, our current sacred cow-word is Modern. Any building labelled modern, however ugly or mistaken, is accepted. But where are our so-called modern Indian styles? Alas, they are mainly poor imitations of other countries' efforts to use present-day materials and techniques. How wonderful it will be when our architects and engineers combine the lessons learned from our own traditional building styles with the honest undisguised use of our regionally plentiful, inexpensive materials. We will be seeing no more plaster imitations of that double joist projection of Japanese post-and-beam construction. The upside-down arches of Brazilia will cease to be badly copied all over our country and the brutal, reinforced concrete blocks of Europe will no longer cost us the unnecessary and wasteful use of precious limited supplies of steel and cement.[9]

Architectural movements in the West have undoubtedly been influenced by the invention of the machine; the mass production of building parts by the mechanized process has played a revolutionary role in not only the development of new forms but in the redefinition of aesthetic theory as well. Consequently, western architects have had to modify and articulate their own position as intermediaries between the available mechanics of construction and the particular requirements of their client.

In cultures where architecture does not spring from the immediate economic and sociological environment, there is a need for architects to rationalize their work in academic terms. To make claims for buildings that are compatible with a prevalent theory or to condemn those that fail to live up to it is a constant refrain of architectural practitioners in the West. However, when the conscious search for a theory behind every act of building becomes the main preoccupation of the architect he becomes the creator of a form determined by his own laws, for his own express purposes.

By contrast, manual sensibilities and the habits of the past still survive in cultures where architecture has not given way to the assembly-line approach. The particular economic conditions of a place, seen in the light

of the professional challenges they pose, tend to produce an architecture with little theoretical or academic basis. Materials and methods are limited, and there is an implicit acknowledgement amongst professionals that the craftsman's role is critical in the making of a building. Beyond that, there is little need to offer polemical justifications.

So, perceiving himself as an architect–craftsman, the architect derives his professional sustenance from outside self-determined bounds. He performs no acts of personal creation but the building he makes does absorb, and suggest, many of the conditions specific to the region. Architecture exists in an effortless continuity determined by tradition and conditioned by natural laws.

For Laurie Baker, the steep slopes of a terracotta roof, protecting the slight patterns of fretwork in a brick wall, convey with faultless clarity the characteristics of the place and time in which it exists. Architecture becomes the medium for a message on local craft, tradition and economy. Baker has always viewed his own role as that of a craftsman. As in the past, there were few specialists; everyone was entitled to build

26

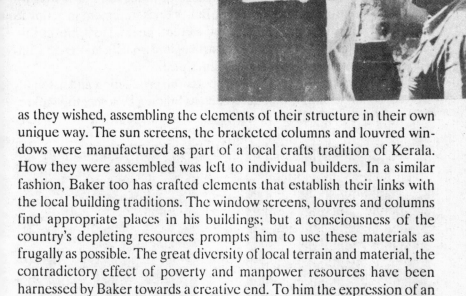

as they wished, assembling the elements of their structure in their own unique way. The sun screens, the bracketed columns and louvred windows were manufactured as part of a local crafts tradition of Kerala. How they were assembled was left to individual builders. In a similar fashion, Baker too has crafted elements that establish their links with the local building traditions. The window screens, louvres and columns find appropriate places in his buildings; but a consciousness of the country's depleting resources prompts him to use these materials as frugally as possible. The great diversity of local terrain and material, the contradictory effect of poverty and manpower resources have been harnessed by Baker towards a creative end. To him the expression of an Indian identity in building is the obvious outcome of these local economic imperatives and lifestyles.

His method of working as designer–builder–contractor in the manner of the traditional master craftsman has, besides extending the conventional role of the architect, produced its own kind of architecture. The building trade has been effectively organized by Baker into teams that have evolved a common approach to design that creates similar elements in assemblies that vary according to the function and scale of each project.

By contrast, modern architecture in urban India has sought to project an expressive vocabulary of surface ornamention based on personal whims and fancies. The treatment of façades, suggesting neither the spaces within the building nor the technology of construction, only tend to make superficial references to the periods of the past in a kind of impoverished, random clutter. The intention is purely ornamental and lacks any contextual unity or any attempt to refer to the actual past. Baker's architecture also uses historical references, but only for reasons of cultural and economic expediency. As a result of this, the continuity of culture gets expressed in building elements and spatial borrowings: a court, a screen wall, a window *jali*. Instead of trying to impose his own stylistic signature upon his buildings, Baker finds fulfilment in acting as a catalyst to his client's functional and cultural needs. He achieves this, almost instinctively, responding to articulated specifications and unspoken, inchoate dictates of the region's past.

Though the architecture that supports the production and assembly of traditional building elements is seen as limiting by some, the making of programmatically diverse buildings by using the same elements estab-

28

lishes links within Baker's own work. The peculiarly local forms of the brick-screen wall, the sloping tile-roof and the overhanging eaves assemble to produce an open plan structure that has distinct climatic and environmental references to their setting in Kerala. Since they are used repeatedly in varying configurations, they maintain a fluid constancy of scale and a human dimension. Baker has built up a vocabulary of these elements over successive projects. These have been arrived at after meticulous research and carefully orchestrated effort.

The successive repetition effectively demonstrates that these elements are the products of a singular ideology and tradition; their inclusion and subsequent transformation into contemporary materials suggests their value as definers of useful space, rather than mere surface ornament. Moreover, their occurrence over several projects also reinforces their importance in the current preoccupation of the profession for a regionally identifiable architecture. By becoming the visible symbols of a transformed tradition they address, with a conclusive directness, the dilemma of contemporary Indian architecture.

The Architect's Home

People in most countries of the world are accusing their architects of failing to produce a modern form of their own previously distinctive architectural styles. If one or two typical modern buildings from each country could be transported and put down in isolation in a large flat desert, could any of us—even architects—walk from one building to another and say 'Ah! Just look at this one—pure Italian' and further on 'My! This is obviously an Indian effort!' A hundred or so years ago we could probably have been successful with such identifications, but there are very grave doubts whether we could do so now.

Fifty years ago we were taught that a building must have an identity. We could certainly tell by looking at a building whether it was domestic or commercial or industrial and so on. It also had its geographical and cultural characteristics. In India there is an incredible wealth of regional architectural styles, and there is not the faintest possibility of confusing one with another. Even where the same materials have been used for building, the climatic and cultural and regional variations are so great that different

methods of construction have been used to produce unique individual
distinctive styles. Furthermore, these distinctive styles apply not only to big
and important buildings but right down to the smallest structures. We can
say that the buildings of any small district are a quintessence of that district's
culture and skill.[10]

Quite obviously the true personality of an architect is reflected in the
way he designs his own house. The design of his house is a manifestation
of his character, principles and architectural beliefs. The personal and
the professional facets of the man blend eloquently on this self-created
territory.

When Laurie and Elizabeth Baker moved to Trivandrum, they bought half-an-acre of land from the Bishop. It seemed, at the time, an unusable purchase: an awkward triangle of stone and scrub, sloping steeply towards the main Nalanchira road. For the Bishop too, the site had been a useless and an impractical acquisition, because it was as unwieldy in plan as it was steep in section; and its stony surface ensured that no bit of green would take hold.

However, Laurie Baker saw such limitations as an architectural challenge; and wishing to have a more permanent foothold in the city, bought the land for a paltry sum of twenty rupees a square metre and moved to Trivandrum.

At first he built only a single-room hut of timber and thatch at the top of the site. It was an inconspicuous structure protected by the shadow of the hill. It housed the Baker library of medical books and also served as a bedroom, living room, dining room and study. Though initially its space might have been adequate for the couple, the temporary nature of its construction obviously was not; and a subsequent monsoon effectively inundated years of accumulated medical papers and journals. Consequently, the first permanent structure, the kitchen building, was made. Built solidly of conventional brick and tile, it made no pretensions to monumentality and was not an aggressive appropriation of the site. 'It was sited,' as Baker says, 'right into the rocks.'

But the growing need for separate living and work areas necessitated an elongated addition of a study. And so a new addition was made following the roof lines of the existing structure, but internally the floor line was decided by the contours of the site. Consequently, the Bakers were always moving across different ground levels, traversing, even on the inside, the natural grades of the site. For almost ten years this house served them adequately and established their physical and spiritual rootedness to the place.

Years later, when Baker's four nieces moved to Trivandrum for a long term of study, he built the 'niecery'—a separate round house on the lower contours. The distance and separation from the main house ensured the Bakers their privacy, and the nieces relative independence.

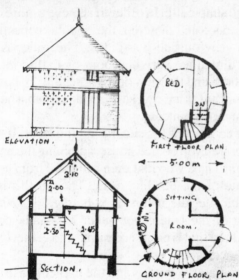

ELEVATION.

FIRST FLOOR PLAN

← 5·00m →

SECTION.

GROUND FLOOR PLAN

FOUNDATION & BASEMENT R.R. IN C.M.
SUPER STRUCTURE - BURNT BRICK IN C.M.
FLOORING - A.C. HOLLOWTILE 4" SLAB 1:2:4
ROOFING - TRADITIONAL TIMBER & M. TILE
DOORS & WINDOWS: JACK WOOD & ANJAL

GROUND FLOOR AREA   19·64 m²
FIRST FLOOR AREA   9·08 m²
TOTAL   AREA   28·72 m²

L. W. BAKER A.R.I.B.A.

'When I began there was hardly a tree on the site,' says Baker, 'but whenever I cut a bit of stone I would pile it up for the retaining walls so all the soil for the retain was either stolen from next door or came from leaves collected and allowed to rot.'

Thus in the course of its occupation the arid rockiness of the site has been transformed into a contoured and less-hostile formation of grass, shrub and coconut plantation. The heavily-shaded areas have surfaced in patterns of stone and lead across changing levels to doorways, mysteriously hidden behind curving walls. Some stepped passageways open suddenly onto a forest thicket, or upward to a view across a valley of coconut palms.

On a site that is quite small, this careful orchestration of contrast—of concealing and revealing, of dark and light, of opening to the landscape at the end of a narrow passage—helps to enrich the feeling of movement through the building, and provide degrees of architectural complexity to an otherwise simple site. In order to achieve a more delicate relationship between space and material, the popular concept of opening the rooms to the view outside is avoided. The valley is not made commonplace by directing every bedroom or bathroom towards it. The valley orientation, and the view of the spreading palms below, becomes decidedly significant as it is revealed through established vantage points, across the frame of a building.

On a lower contour of the site, facing the trees, is a recent addition to the complex—a two-roomed house, adjoining the niecery. It was built for Baker's son, Tilak, who had then returned from college. He is now managing some of the building work. Though this is the fifth major addition on the site, the incursion is hardly felt. With his instinctive understanding of the landscape, Baker has managed to confine this building to an area that is easily accessible and yet secluded by the heavy foilage that conceals it.

Much of the material for this and the earlier constructions has come from rather unconventional sources. 'They were pulling down an old boat jetty, down the coast, in order to make a new bridge. All the tiles were going to be fed into the new foundations; but I managed to salvage some and bring them for the house,' says Baker. Even the front door and some windows have come from very old houses that have long since been demolished.

By making such insertions into his plans, it is not only the preservation of antiques that is the concern of Baker—but also its active re-use, even as fragments, in new buildings. This re-application of old pieces reveals that Baker understands architectural history as a continuing process. In appropriating history for his own work, he relocates the past in the present landscape, suggesting not a static preservation but an active recall and celebration of antiquity.

This honest appreciation of materials and textures has produced a house close to its natural state—brick, stone and wood left unspoilt and unconcealed. The determination of the requisite material for a requisite purpose comes from a natural instinct to conserve.

...oom addition....

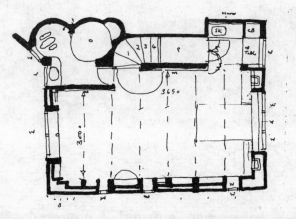

Standing on top of the hill, looking out across the rooftops to the valley below, the Hamlet, the name given to the Baker home, appears like an architectural museum—a record of the past twenty years of the history of building in Kerala. The changing roofs, their structure and texture,

terracotta fish-tile roofs

the doors and windows, embody the change in materials and technology that has occurred over the years—the earlier structures being of wood and fish tile, the more recent ones of cement and Mangalore tile. In a market situation over which Baker has little control, adaptation to new materials has become a natural recourse.

Even the journey to Baker's house through the city is a symbolic return to the origins, a transformation to another architectural age; it takes the visitor from the denser concrete centre of Trivandrum, through the freshness and shade of the suburbs, to the relatively unspoilt outskirts of Nalanchira. The house is not visible from the road, and the walk up towards it is one of discovery and accidental encounters—an entrance gate, a steeper gradient along a workshop to a free-standing door, a curved path along the circular niecery and the final flight of steps leading to the plinth of the main house. The house itself, open but benign, is oriented towards the countryside—away from the city—and so it renews its links to the past, to its Kerala ancestry. The visitor hardly ever notices the extent of the constructions, for the house has been effectively fragmented to follow the contours, so that the rooms rise with the land. Bits of the house—portico, study, bedroom, dining and kitchen—come together under the dense foliage of tropical trees and shrubs. Terracotta roofs and red brick walls, stained by the monsoons, blend quietly into the forest background.

In the relatively affluent Trivandrum the Bakers continue to live their lives just as they had in the frugal setting of Pithoragarh in the Himalayas. Only the setting has changed. A different climate, a strikingly different terrain and vegetation, and a more urbane clientele has failed to alter the Bakers' simple and plain lifestyle.

A subdued delicacy, even a kind of domestic elegance, is attained as the interiors and furnishing are designed on the basis of the desired domestic activity; furniture and machines are accommodated or intimately scaled to reflect their order in the housekeeping. That cooking, eating and washing are the shared family activities of the kitchen is suggested in the central placement of stoves, tables and the sink.

Rooms do not follow the conventional classifications of a house. The family eats in the kitchen under a ceiling hung with pots and pans. These create a useful decoration for the space while taking care of the kitchen's storage needs. A formal dining room does not exist. If a visitor

37

the veranda....

opens to the palm-fringed countryside

is present he or she eats with the family under the ceiling of kitchen utensils. Even the wiring is not juggled or concealed. It sits comfortably atop a projecting brick course above eye level and enters the sockets along the walls. Bulbs hang off simple wooden brackets.

The severely plain and the unusually commodious plan is typical of Baker's style. Its relationships and room sizes, its use of natural light and ventilation, built-in seating and storage, simply pegged wooden doors and windows, all express the convictions of Laurie Baker's architectural beliefs. The striking austerity of the interiors perhaps again demonstrates a deeply-felt yearning for a Quaker absoluteness and order. It is as if any undue decoration would distract from the dignity of the pure forms.

A comprehension of the possibilities of using simple workmanship to create architectural settings is, according to Baker, the best possible way of ordering a domestic environment. This ideal has been pursued through a strict consistency in the designs for institutional buildings, housing for the poor, as well as private residences for the affluent. The production and assembly of individual segments of a building by hand, and through honest industry, may have its origins in a Quaker ideology; but it also makes ample sense in a world of diminishing local resources and plentiful labour.

Buildings and Practice

I can never understand an architect who designs 500 houses all exactly the same. It doesn't take much to put all the components into at least half-a-dozen other combinations. It's perfectly easy to mix materials on any given site so the possibilities for variety are endless. . . If only we didn't level sites, and eliminate trees but instead plan to go around them, then we wouldn't get the long monotonous rows to begin with. . . .

Most materials have their own special characteristics and if used honestly and simply they contribute to the 'looks' of a building merely from their colour, their texture and the patterns formed by joining them together. There is no need to cover them over with costly finishes. Let a brick wall look like a brick wall and a stone wall look like a stone wall. Concrete should look like concrete and not be plastered or painted to look like marble.[11]

The project that is the most representative of Baker's architecture is the Centre for Development Studies (p.160) in Trivandrum. All the concerns of his architectural practice—the sensitivity to the natural contours and elements of a site, the honest and optimum utilization of the materials—find an expression in the plan and structures of the Centre. The buildings of this Centre also incorporate all the elements characteristic of Baker's style—the *jalis*, the traditional roofs, the stepped arches, the overhanging eaves and the skylights. The design of the Centre for Development Studies demonstrates how Baker is able to transform vernacular architecture to suit the requirements of a modern academic institution.

Established in 1965 to promote economic development in the state, the eminent economists of the Centre sought to project its socially-conscious goals in an appropriately progressive architecture, and Baker was the obvious choice as the architect. The project became a testing ground for many of the ideas he had experimented with previously on a domestic scale. In designing the buildings of the Centre—the library, classrooms, offices and houses—the absence of precise topographical surveys and existing plantation plans necessitated that much of the design-work be

carried out on the site itself. Apart from preparing plans for individual buildings on paper, the more difficult task was to find suitable locations for these on the site itself.

The numerous changing levels of the completed academic complex, is the result of plotting the plans on the natural terraces of the terrain. Consequently, to a visitor, the buildings of the Centre never appear as a singular forbidding entity. The varying levels of the site fragment the complex into its individual components, each in its own landscape, created by groves of existing trees and foliage.

Kerala's tropical climate has been kind to Baker's buildings in a way it seldom is to modern uni-style structures, and Baker, in turn, has been kind to nature. The location of virtually every tree and sapling on a site is taken into account before the building location is chosen, and rarely, if ever, is a contour disturbed, or a plant removed. This is partly due to Baker's frugality ('I think it's a waste of money to level a well-moulded site,' he says), and partly due to his regard for nature.

jali walls of the library....

The site plan also makes a clear demarcation between vehicular and pedestrian routes; the heavy cutting of the site for major roads is confined to the lower slopes while walkways meander along the upper contours. The variations and folds of the roof, too, seen from a distance, do not appear to be the outcome of whimsical expression but suggest, by their very shape and size, the importance of the functions housed within. Casting shadows on the lower roofs the composition intentionally suggests a protective family of buildings. On the whole, the forms that are so skilfully distributed over the site, merge with the landscape to provide elegant proof of the belief that the creative process embodies a complete understanding of physical and environmental laws.

Baker achieves both a natural economy in cost and a subtle variation in design by the way he treats his building material during the process of construction. On a rocky terrain the rock itself becomes the foundation for building, but where a footing is required random rubble is brought together in a mixture of lime, sand and cement. The brick walls that sit directly on it are assembled in a variation of bonds and mortar mixes that are absolutely essential to support the roof load. No material is wasted. Where a single brick thickness is necessary, where a half will do, where water seepage may occur—are questions and concerns that find their resolution on the site, as the building goes up. The final expression is an outcome of this meticulous attention to structural and economic detail.

Concrete is used very sparingly, often in a folded-slab design with waste and discarded tiles used as fillers, thereby making the roof light and inexpensive. Innovative bonding techniques for brick allow Baker to build walls of only a half-brick thickness. In many cases they are stepped and curved for added rigidity. The interiors too are uncompromisingly direct and simple, devoid of superfluous clutter, expensive veneers or flashy details. Baker often eliminates and sometimes modifies glass windows, frames and sills, preferring small openings in brick, like the traditional *jali* which fragments the harsh sunlight and permits the breeze to blow through a building. Where large openings are required, he corbels in bricks securing the doors directly to the wall surface.

A characteristic feature of Baker's work is the *jali*, a perforated screen made of bricks with a surface of tiny regular openings in the wall, producing intricate patterns of light and shadow. In Baker's hands the *jali* becomes the true vernacular solution to the problem of the window, and it has the elegance and simplicity which the traditional craftsman would consider appropriate. It catches light and air and diffuses glare while allowing for privacy and security—combining the functions of a window and a ventilator. A *jali* opening encourages air flow, yet the construction of this form of cross-ventilation requires neither special materials nor special skills.

Baker maintains that the simplest and most economical spanning of

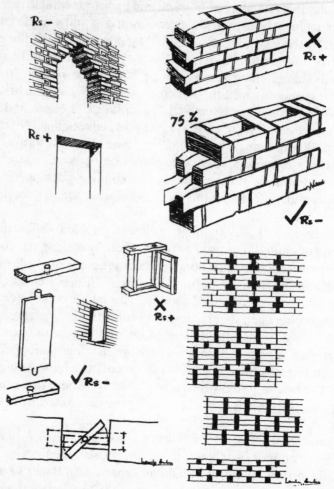

an opening in a brick wall is to use the 'stepped arch' or the 'corbelled arch', where the bricks on each course are cantilevered out a few inches beyond the course below, until the span is bridged. If a rectangular opening is desired, a form of reinforced brickwork can be used which capitalizes on the composite action of the lintel with the masonry above.

The single most costly item in a building is the roof, accounting for about one-third of the total cost. A pitched roof made of Mangalore tiles typical of Kerala's fine old buildings, is as much a part of the landscape of the region as the palm tree, and was used from the humblest house to the palace of the former Maharaja of Travancore.

In the palm-fringed, tropical landscape of the region, Baker has managed to re-create the traditional roof but in a contemporary rendition. The Mangalore tile of the vernacular is relieved of its accepted function of cover and is introduced into the folded concrete slab as a filler in order to lighten the roof weight and eliminate the use of scarce timber. The resulting form has the shape of a traditional roof with its overhanging eaves and skylights but without the expense of traditional labour and construction.

Baker's architecture also interprets traditional patterns of thermal design in a contemporary idiom. An example of this is seen in the recent addition of a computer centre to the twenty-five-year-old campus of the Centre for Development Studies.(p.171). The housing of sophisticated computers required strict environmental controls of temperature, lighting and air flow. But paradoxically, the site—a prominent location on the campus—also required that the building correspond and respect the open elevations of the library and hostels nearby. Baker offered an effective double-wall solution which duplicated on the outer surface the neighbouring patterns of brick, but produced on the inside the volume required of a sophisticated laboratory. The residual space, created by the meeting of these two shells, houses the offices and storage, and provides a thermal seal between the inside and the outside. Nearby, at the canteen for the Centre, high latticed brick walls and a pond are used to draw air across its surface and cool the building—an interpretive re-creation of a traditional cooling system.

By gently stepping up the singly-loaded buildings at the Centre, Baker attempts to create continuous sophisticated breezeways to temper the humid climate in a deceptively simple way. In this, as in so many other areas, his skilful manipulation of the natural elements to create the desired thermal comfort is in direct contrast to the contemporary architectural practices which seek to impose control on nature by shutting it out with glass and concrete walls, and the use of artificial ventilation and temperature control systems.

I've been brought up with the idea that they, engineers, are one of the people you can consult if you're in a hole or if you are designing something special,

45

but now we think of air-conditioning as something you apply to a building.
You run a duct through a false ceiling or stick a box in the window, but the
architect no longer cares. He knows if he can't do something he can always
fall back on the mechanical engineer or the structures man.[12]

In every aspect of this project Baker's architecture is characterized
by an approach that has shed all preconceived design ideas. In the
residential complex for the Centre, he planned a group of homes whose
design stemmed from the specific needs of those who were to inhabit
them.

Senior officers who usually get large, well-equipped houses with plenty of
rooms, more often than not have only a small family and in fact need a
spacious room for entertaining rather than a number of rooms for their
small family. At the other end of the scale, it is very often the peons and
drivers who have large families and other dependents too. Certainly the
middle section of the institution's workers have several children and often
parents and unmarried brothers and sisters living with them. All this means
that the usual pattern of accommodation provided in an institution is not at
all what is actually needed. At the Centre for Development Studies, therefore, the housing has been designed to meet these actual needs and we find
that the houses for the peons, etc. are comparatively spacious buildings with
three reasonable-sized living rooms (all rooms become bedrooms at night),

46

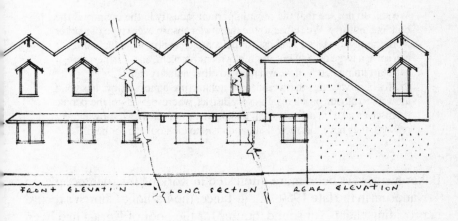

FRONT ELEVATION · LONG SECTION · REAR ELEVATION

two small bathrooms, a kitchen which has enough space also for eating, a store room, and a large work area.[13]

Another building, the State Institute of Languages (p.189), demonstrates Baker's resolve to work within the severe limitations of government finance. Like the Centre for Development Studies, the state's intention to extend education in the local vernacular required a sizeable building where translation into the native languages would be carried out, and, subsequently, printed for distribution to various districts. Though the work had already been entrusted to the Public Works Department(PWD), their estimate of Rs 2,00,000 for just the first phase, was more than the funds available for the entire project. It was then that Baker's intervention was sought by the then Chief Minister, Achuta Menon, to suggest a more reasonable alternative; and, in the end, despite persistent opposition from the PWD, Baker's proposal for a simple but permanent shed-like architecture of exposed brickwork was built at one-fifth the original estimate of the first phase!

Baker's work has been often referred to as the architecture of marginality as his designs make optimum use of available funds and materials. The lower middle class forms the bulk of his urban clients. Yet the impetus to work for the poor does not come from any consciousness to promote development—the main idea behind the hi-tech buildings and prefabricated techniques of today. Baker maintains that high technology and prefabrication make little sense in a country that still has a largely under-employed labour force.

> We still do not see that the most important industry in the country is the building industry. We refuse to see that it can absorb every type of worker from the highly-skilled scientist to the completely non-skilled labourer. It can solve a large area of our unemployment problem, and, furthermore, it can start immediately, if we will it, as no other industry can.
>
> My observation is that vernacular architecture almost always has good answers to all our problems. In every district, wherever you go, the people themselves take an active part in making their houses. Now, for whatever reasons, they have lost their skills, and need to look outside for help.[14]

Baker has always been more interested in working for such people. In Trivandrum in the late 1960s, for instance, the Catholic Church's record in providing cheap, yet sound, houses for the poor of Kerala had been

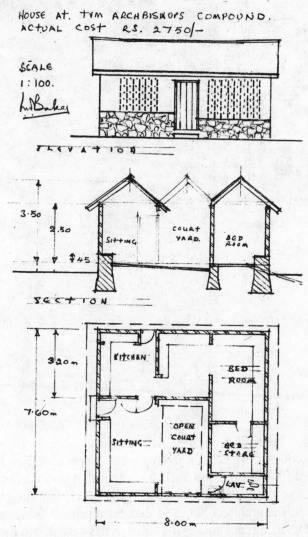

HOUSE At. TVM ARCHBISHOPS COMPOUND.
ACTUAL COST RS. 2750/-

SCALE
1 : 100.

ELEVATION

3·50
2.30
·45

Sitting   COURt
            YARD.   BED
                      ROOM

SECTION

3·20 m

7·60 m

KITCHEN   BED
                ROOM

SITTING   OPEN
          COURT
          YARD   BED
                  STORE
                  LAV.

8·00 m

dismal. Local engineers and builders, after years of planning, had failed to provide anything more than two or three expensive houses.

In an experiment to assess whether it was in fact possible to build cheaply and appropriately, Archbishop Mar Gregorios invited Baker to demonstrate his techniques of low-cost construction in a convincing way by allowing him to build for different congregations. Baker's first com-

49

Namboodripad house....

mission for the church was designed as a forty square metre house built around a courtyard(p.80). Its arrangement of space allowed for privacy between different areas, in such a manner that the different activities in the house did not intrude upon each other. For the greater part of the year, the architect believed that extra private living space could be added to such small houses if a courtyard is designed in the centre of the house. The house was ready within two weeks for less than the cost specified by the church and within the income range of the poorest family. Constructed of exposed brick and a Mangalore tile roof, the tiny jewel-like building still sits—almost twenty years later—undamaged and inconspicuous under the shadow of a gnarled neem tree. Its low entrance under the gable of a now-stained terracotta roof reveals the light of an internal court surrounded by a series of small whitewashed rooms.

Baker's success with this project for the Archbishop prompted a number of unique commissions. 'I still get calls,' he says, 'From people who say I have a small plot of land, four thousand rupees, a wife and seven children, a brother and sister-in-law, and old parents who can't walk upstairs. I need a house. Will you build it for me?'

Amongst the best of Baker's early houses was for one such client. Namboodripad, a non-gazetted officer with a typical meagre government income. 'Mr Baker,' he had asked, 'I need a six-bedroom house, but I have only ten thousand rupees; can you do it?' Baker thought about it for a moment and agreed. Whereupon Namboodripad pulled out the notes from his pocket and handed them over. Whether or not the exchange between the architect and the client happened as dramatically as that, one thing is certain—for a teacher a three-storeyed six-bedroom house, built at one-fifth the cost of a conventional house, was reason enough for celebration (p.86). In the Namboodripad house, Baker's response to a small plot, that sloped steeply towards a stream, was to keep the building compact, retaining the natural character of the site. The plan evolved out of two intersecting circles—the smaller becoming a stair, the larger dividing to form the living area on the ground and six bedrooms on the two floors above.

The first principle of an affordable Baker house is always the use of local materials appropriate to the climate. Brick, tile, lime, palm thatch, stone, granite and laterite (which are found abundantly in Kerala) and country timber usually replace steel and glass in a Baker building. Not only are they more suited to the hot humid climate, but they also minimize the use of non-renewable resources and maximize local employment by encouraging small-scale industry.

We have already forgotten that many of our big old irrigation and power dams, which still serve us efficiently, were built with lime mortar and knew nothing about cement. By developing economic, simple, widespread lime production units we could solve many unemployment problems and produce fine, efficient, versatile building material with tremendous savings

51

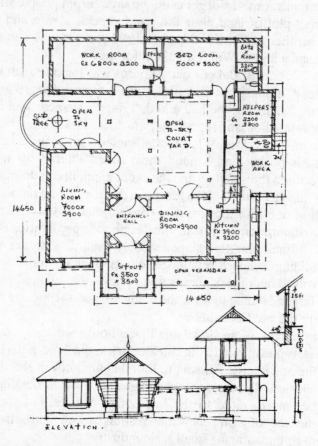

ELEVATION.

...n building costs and energy throughout the land. It is only necessary for us to go one step further with the research work which our forefathers have done—that is for us to *add on* our twentieth century contribution to *improve* on what has already been achieved. But it must be a contribution and not a contradiction or a confrontation.[15]

ancestral remnants make gate and

entrance porch

Baker's ability to consistently build structures of lasting value at a low cost is reason enough for low-income families to accept his methods of cost-reducing technology. For the Namboodripads and hundreds of others, caught in the unaffordable maze of conventional practice, Baker offers the only sensible alternative.

In executing these ideas Baker works closely with a small team of masons and carpenters trained in his own workshop. Almost all his buildings have been built under his personal supervision; from the laying of the foundation to the fabrication of metal grilles for windows, his involvement remains intense and inexhaustible.

An important feature of Baker's cost-saving methods is his attitude of

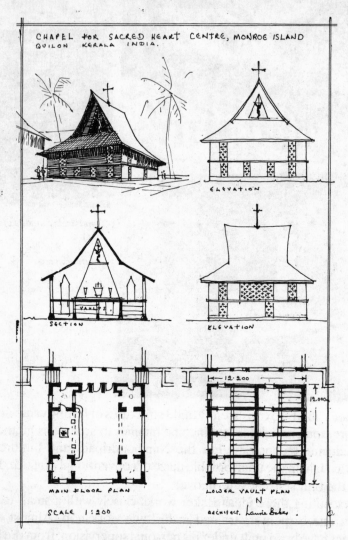

CHAPEL for SACRED HEART CENTRE, MONROE ISLAND
QUILON KERALA INDIA.

ELEVATION

SECTION

ELEVATION

VAULTS

MAIN FLOOR PLAN

LOWER VAULT PLAN

SCALE 1:200

architect. Laurie Baker.

12.200

12.000

N

restraint and a willingness to incorporate existing materials in new structures. In no project is the feature of re-application more apparent than in the Narayanan House(p.110) in Trivandrum. Mrs. Narayanan had a large quantity of old timber—much of it saved from an old house which had been pulled down. Door frames were too small to be re-used as

54

doors—they were converted into windows. No attempt was made at any sort of reconstruction or reproduction of an old type house; Baker merely made use of the timber to fit the needs of the new plan. 'This does not,' he says, 'violate the historic integrity of the old materials because the relics continue to be appreciated in the new setting. Salvage acquires meaning by juxtaposition.'

Indeed the old meets the new in surprising ways. Wooden remnants of the ancestral home—now torn down—are comfortably incorporated into the new house. An antique gateway, complete with door and letter-holder becomes a focus within the modern boundary wall. The main porch beyond is itself a curious mix of the traditional and the contemporary. Its massive, heavily-bracketed columns, the panelled ebony doorway with its dense, immovable bulk—these memorable pieces of an old building now become focal points of the modern structure. The old structures do not merely provide ornamentation, but participate functionally and harmoniously with the modern setting.

That a particular artifact belongs exclusively to a specific time is perhaps too static a view of architectural history. To Baker, architecture represents the collective memory of a people and is expressed through the re-establishment of historical fragments, gateways and ancient columns in contemporary settings, thereby offering new interpretations of the past.

Students of architecture who have worked with Baker are struck by his remarkable capacity to improvise. Baker avoids cumbersome working drawings which detail the building for the contractor. Instead, he improvises on the site itself and so incorporates any available usable material—whether bricks or electrical fixtures—into the design. To the residents of Trivandrum, it is not such an odd sight to find the elderly Baker rummaging through junkyards in search of discarded doors and windows. One rare find was the portico of a temple demolished in one part of Trivandrum which became the formal entrance to the Chitralekha Studio Complex (p.192), because of its ornamental woodwork.

Baker's interest in finding an appropriate response to each site condition makes his presence essential during the construction. The organic symbiosis between floor line and terrain, tree and wall, building volume and landscape, window and view is achieved only by his constant intervention during every phase of construction. Improvisations are made to suit the life-pattern of each client. The placing of an ironing board, the position of the family idol or the literary acquisition of an intellectual—all become a part of the process of a constructive decision. The subtle modulations of surfaces and textures, the variation in wall and window heights, and their seemingly simple placement would not be possible in drafting-room architecture.

Architecture begins in the realm of ideas and drawings, and ends in a tangible structure—the realization of the idea. Though several architects produce attractive sketches and drawings of an intensely personal nature, few architects today consider the medium of drawing as a means of communication. However, for Baker drawing is a significant working medium, where the process of transformation becomes a testing ground for his imagination, his perception of the client's requirements, and his own interpretation of history. Though he draws only that which is absolutely essential—often in free-hand sketches which are

Narayanan house....

later formalized for the builders—it gives a substantial insight into his thoughts and are a testimony to the fact that the end result is not different from the original conception. A thumbnail sketch for the house of a dancer (p.110) has the same quality of spiralling playfulness that characterizes the actual building.

Like the designs which are done in close coordination with the client, the drawing also adjusts to the message it is meant to convey. For the Cathedral at Tiruvella (p.183), Baker had produced a set of gaudy water-colours because 'the Bishop could follow these more directly than the plan'. For the Chapel at Ooty, drawings were done with the idea of suggesting different alternatives for saving the trees in the heavily-wooded site.

Moreover, the attention paid to the particular needs of an individual and how these may be accommodated within specified budgets give a unique character to each space. In his view, the specific task of an architect includes not only providing basic shelter to his clients, but also necessarily taking into account their accumulations, peculiarities, obsessions and specific requirements. If the home for a dancer becomes a makeshift auditorium at the time of informal performances, that of an antique-collector becomes a small gallery; if one client requires numerous brick-beds for an extended family, they are built as easily as shelving for another who may have an equally large collection of traditional figurines. For the owner, a self-occupied home, designed, built and lived-in assumes the status of an institution permanently rooted, which he expects never to leave. And Baker's painstaking thoroughness to detail and the scientific adaptability of all the furnishings makes it eminently suitable for a single set of residents. Though this attention to detail and his initiating an alternative craft tradition require more than just isolated examination of specific examples, the sophisticated workmanship evident in his buildings needs to be viewed from the perspective of the architecture of Kerala, and of his functioning within difficult material and economic constraints.

Kerala's architecture of specific local materials assembled in a particular climate and within the cultural traditions peculiar to the state, makes it virtually impossible to extend Baker's one-man methods to the rest of the country. Yet a widespread application of the principles he has evolved are universally applicable for virtually any type of building anywhere in India.

Baker's principles and ideologies naturally produce an architecture that is modern in its purest sense: having simple and minimal construction and utilizing only those materials that are absolutely essential for enclosure. However, his multi-purpose planning takes into consideration the fact that lifestyles change over the life span of a building.

In the Menon house (p.112) this multi-functional consideration is expressed in an open, free form plan adjusted to the irregular plot. The concept of privacy—or rather that of the isolated bedrooms—is discarded in preference for rooms that are all interconnected and do not conform to any particular shape. Walls splay out unexpectedly and their surface is broken in a fretwork pattern of little squares, rectangles and crosses, creating a lattice screen common to many of Baker's houses. The thin, 'witch's-cap' roof (Baker's term for a roof resembling a witch's cap) stretches to cover the house like a taut tarpaulin of concrete. The asymmetry and folds on its surface allow the skylights to bring in a bit of the sky and the sun to the shaded confines below.

Baker's concern for the needs of each family extends from the private houses he has built to institutions and to low-cost group housing as well. His plan prototype for the fishermen's homes outside Trivandrum (p.202) is developed out of the plan of the original hut lost to the cyclone. The new construction is designed to preserve the traditions and customs of the fishermen and at the same time to raise their hygienic standards. This is done with local materials, and a passive cooling system, made possible by staggering the buildings on the site plan. In each house the interior courtyard is designed to generate convective air currents and induce a cool breeze through the interior. The building elements are suitably assembled and modified on a common plan so as to fulfil individual requirements.

> One way of demonstrating to the poor that low-cost building doesn't mean poor quality is to do similar things for the rich. Though I've never felt the need to demonstrate this because they (the poor) know the value of money, they can understand cost-reduction principles better than the middle class. And they are very open to new ideas or adjustments, because they are always

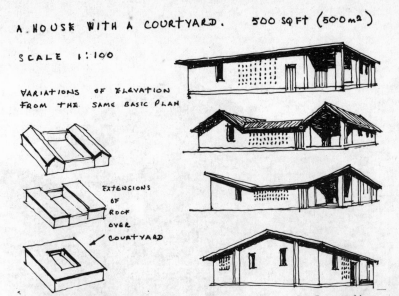

A HOUSE WITH A COURTYARD.   500 SQ FT (50·0 m²)

SCALE 1:100

VARIATIONS OF ELEVATION
FROM THE SAME BASIC PLAN

EXTENSIONS
OF
ROOF
OVER
COURTYARD

trying to make a little money go as far as possible. So whether I wanted it or not I got into low-cost design.[16]

The attention he pays to each house and to each inhabitant as an individual client, has prompted Baker to accept fewer large-scale commissions. A family's attachment to their place of dwelling, their sense of security and familiarity is what Baker nurtures.

The gentle probing of their lives, the psychology of each family, combined with a careful scrutiny of their physical requirements allows the architect to arrive at a series of plan choices: a traditional house with the court as its centre; a round plan organized around the family room; a curving form with rooms dispersed along a hill; or a compact tower-house on a tight site. The alternatives Baker offers are numerous and suggest to the client that beyond the practical aspects of construction the choices are entirely his own. The empathy and deep involvement he experiences in the designing of every home gives him an acute comprehension of the setting and the nature of a home.

When, the Alexanders, a retired couple, require space for themselves and an appropriate setting for their furniture, assiduously collected over the forty years of service, Baker offers an apt solution (p.101). At the same time he responds to the needs of the Namboodripad couple who have little by way of accumulated goods, but live in an extended family

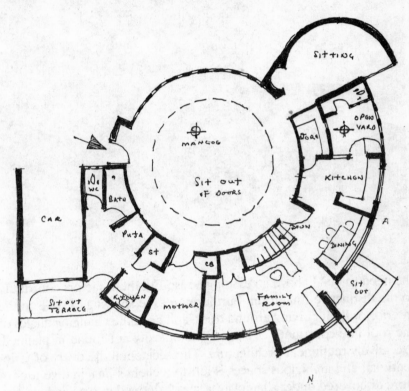

(p. 86). He understands the ways in which certain details in a home are distinctive to each individual; they become, in a way, the generic symbols of the place. A kennel built as an integral part of the house, a niche in the entrance wall for the morning bottle of milk—these are the kind of minor deviations that are possible in an architecture that is constantly adjusting to personal and private idiosyncracies.

One of Baker's professional concerns is the extension of the inhabited territory of a home into accidental and immeasurable realms. This intention arises from the architect's wish to give the client more than the conventional spaces required of a house and to transform the external site conditions to suit its design. These deviations from the norm are the result of the decisive characteristics of the site itself—an ancient mango tree, a rocky outcrop, an architecturally severe slope, or

61

the need to build above an existing house. All these factors contribute to the distinctive final form. Furthermore, the splaying of walls in the interior or their curving around trees, and even the changing angles of the roof line contribute to a spatial complexity not found in planned, excessively-rectilinear architecture. The accidental discovery of unintentional and ambigious spaces is left to a client's imaginative use—a store discovered under a stairway, a seat fashioned into a window.

The eventual inclusion of all that makes one site different from another and allows for a more natural appreciation of individuality has little to do with ideology or stylistic self-expression. Practising within strict constraints of function and economy, the peculiar plasticity that Baker achieves in the interiors and architectural lyricism is the outcome of functions adapted and finely juxtaposed. An unplastered bedroom of brick is lit by the dark stained louvres of a traditional window; another window is recessed into an alcove—a tiny room in its own right. Such spaces allow the ordinary to become exceptional—and in so doing extend the mind to a multitude of varying associations. Where the effect of light or dark, heat or cold, air and shadow are constantly being altered, the house becomes a tactile and sensuous place—where patterns of sunlight are reflected on the walls;

where the simple act of reading is elevated by the architectural detail of enclosing a seat by the window. Terraces and verandas between rooms—spaced of no measurable consequence—allow the occupant to discover new uses in a continual exchange with the building.

The need for contact with the outside and with the organic profile of the site leads Baker to introduce architectural elements that express this duality of inside and out, of man-made and natural. The screen wall is made of brick and also by the absence of it; the courtyard is a delineated enclosure but is also open to the sky—both are at once outside as well as inside. Such spatial and building elements are used to suggest sequences of habitation in varying plans. In the Vaidyanathan house (p. 98), for instance, the circular screen not only conceals the private residence from the outside but also establishes a link with it. The enclosing court is not viewed just as a residual space between rooms but is consciously made and appreciated as an outdoor enclosure. In the Aniruddhin house (p. 84), the resident's orientation is inwards to a more utilitarian courtyard in the centre.

The design of the spaces for an intimate, personal and familial occupation are the characteristics that mark all of Laurie Baker's domestic architecture. It is this attention to every detail of living pat-

terns and habits that makes it extremely difficult for Baker to build for an anonymous mass of people. But this does not keep him from trying. When a fishermen's village near Trivandrum was washed away by a cyclone, Baker was asked by the state government to prepare plans for its rehabilitation(p. 202). The project took him into the field for an extensive survey of each family's requirement. After erecting a uniform shell for each family, he accommodated their specific and individual needs in custom-built insertions—a task that required as much time and effort as is needed for any of the projects of the middle-class clients.

The specifics of design which distinguish a home and set it apart from its neighbours are as essential in low-cost housing for the poor as they are in the homes of the affluent. Baker's understanding of this aspect of human nature leaves no room for skimping or compromise, regardless of who the client is. Bureaucrats, funding and supervising low-cost housing projects, are always surprised at his genuine personal involvement, which they consider unnecessary for vast housing schemes.

The basic conflict between bureaucratic thinking and Baker's approach invariably remains—where one tries to establish similarities in design, the other tries to discover distinctions between individual families and their needs. Such an approach is perhaps related to a desire to create places of rootedness—a permanance lacking in the anonymous and transient structures provided by the government.

Though his clients rarely participate in the actual construction of their building, the evolving nature of a Baker design and the absence of decisive blueprints for a building demonstrate the participatory nature of the design process. This allows the client to get an 'on site' feel for his home and permit him changes and additions that may not have been possible under conventional conditions. Such participation has been particularly beneficial in the larger bureaucratic schemes for mass-housing where the assembly-line approach has produced repetitive pattern of anonymous buildings. Baker's style of architecture proves that there is a viable, practicable and appealing alternative.

Taken together, Baker's projects suggest the development of a highly-skilled and practical perception of space, material and construction technology. Beyond their immediate design resolutions, they exhibit commitments and ideas that have absorbed the architect through the course of his lifetime. Though each building naturally varies in site conditions, programme, and details of design, collectively, they manifest many similarities and a set of architectural constants. In the disposition of their plans, their ordering of the public and private realms, their consistency of natural texture as the only surface ornament, their particular geometric unity or sequential fluency, they demonstrate the determination and the continually experimenting and expansive will of the man who has created them.

A Creative Contribution

Simplicity, order and regularity—these are the factors that guide Baker's search for design integrity. If an architect's contribution to society be looked upon as the public's perception of him as a socially responsible professional, and his work as a socially responsible act, then most of Baker's contemporaries have deliberately forsaken this responsibility in favour of wealthier clients and larger commissions. Surrounded by professionals of questionable ethics and standards, Baker's contribution has become even more significant. The moral responsibility to set examples of fine craftsmanship and utility, and to achieve more within greater constraints, is the true craftsman's attitude towards his work, however big or small. The same, painstaking view to details that has gone into creating the vast complex of buildings for the Centre for Development Studies (p.160), can be seen in the design of a towel-rack for the Alexander house (p.101).

The architecture of tradition changes the concept of individual creativity into collective expression. A critical factor in interpreting Baker's contribution is not to judge the originality of a single work in conventional terms, but to see each in the continuum of the architect's work of a lifetime. In such architecture no one work is greater than another; and if indeed qualitative comparisons need to be established, buildings can only be judged on the inadequate modern basis of function, size and budget.

Baker's return to the traditional has little in common with a romantic's preference for the primitive life. His use of local tile and brick is not to be viewed as an expedient stylistic device. It stems from his desire to conserve and the need to elaborate and extend the architectural tradition to the modern designs. The result is an optimum use of scarce materials. The dramatic reduction of building cost, the proportionate increase in habitable space, and the environmental efficiency and thermal comfort that follow, are, in Baker's scheme of things, the key concerns in building.

Though Baker has a formidable body of buildings to his credit, his work is clearly out of the contemporary Indian or international mainstream. This is largely so because the problems of the poorer clients and their subsequent resolution into 'marginal' architecture arouse little concern amongst the media. Moreover, successful solutions to problems of low-cost housing are viewed as a threat to a profession that survives on financially lucrative projects. Baker's efforts at economizing are bound to be met with stiff resistance in a system where architectural fees are calculated as a percentage of the building costs. Yet, the single-mindedness with which he has sought his vision of building, his dedication to the practice, his unwillingness to compromise on quality, have made him a kind of legend among his peers. He has forcefully illustrated the importance of principles and how their application to building can offer numerous solutions—besides his own—to the urgent housing problems of the country.

Because Baker falls outside of the professional mainstream, it is perhaps unfair to assess his work in an international or a national context. Yet to the younger architects of his adopted country and his home state of Kerala, his work offers a narrower, more focussed relevance. The sheer magnitude of his work makes him an important figure in Indian architecture. His enduring presence in India, the four decades of a practice sustained in the same place, has had its impact—if not directly on the profession, at least on the countless numbers of rural clients touched by his concerns.

Yet, the message of Baker's professional life is there in his buildings for all to see. His genius has been most effectively articulated in an architecture of structural honesty based on the culture of its setting. Rejecting values alien to the place, wasteful building practices and self-seeking ethics of the architectural profession, Baker has devised his own architecture and his own morally-satisfying way of practising it. His singular ambition of a better building at lesser cost made him eliminate

useless members of the conventional architectural team just the way he eliminated unnecessary material from a building. Baker's most impressive achievement has doubtlessly been his ability to construct suitable buildings at low cost and so direct bureaucrats and politicians to the growing needs of the poor. Over the course of a thousand-odd buildings he has clearly demonstrated this concern with unwavering confidence and firmness. The source for all his professional work has always remained his own particular brand of Quaker humanism, which, more than any single structure, is his most significant legacy to architecture.

Architects and critics have drawn parallels between Baker and the work of Hassan Fathy of Egypt, who, like Baker, had spent virtually a lifetime promoting traditional skills in his own buildings. But what appears ironic is that while Fathy's buildings rose to support and revive an ancient craft tradition, Baker's are the instinctive outcome of local economics and environmental conditions. Moreover, while Fathy's work and ideas—despite worldwide recognition—have been ridiculed in his own country, Baker's are slowly being appreciated in his adopted country.

There are also striking similarities in their work. Both have taken on the role of architectural crusaders. Both consider themselves as only brief sparks in the light of historical continuity. Both have expressed this belief through the education and training of craftsmen, and the reorientation of their craft to contemporary purpose—the methodical inculcation of pride of labour and quality which they felt necessary in order to systematically uncover all but forgotten techniques of construction.

But while Fathy's buildings have been looked upon as those of an eccentric and an incurable nostalgic, Baker's buildings have an aura of quiet assurance, which comes as much from their economic expediency as from their expressive strength—the ability to transform traditional ideas into a wholly contemporary usage.

At a time when India and Indian architecture is passing through a particularly difficult phase, turning from rampant industrial growth to one of controlled social development, Baker's ideas are becoming increasingly relevant. His realization of the need for low-cost shelter and his practical and sensitive solutions have made him an unlikely doyen amongst a younger generation of more socially-conscious architects. A new minority of architects and social planners have begun to view architecture as a catalyst for change, and the apparent need to evolve new buildings in accordance with the aspirations of the vast majority. They echo Baker's view that there is no alternative to vernacular, frugal architecture.

> There's no oil, our forests are already denuded of wood; we have coal reserves only for another thirty years and with this high-tech stuff, nobody has been able to come up with solutions that are energy-conserving both in the production of materials, and how they are assembled.[17]

However, in spite of so many years of continuous and diverse practice, Baker has not succeeded in creating a national following. Private non-profit and voluntary organizations have only marginally benefited from his ideas. Exploiting his techniques for their housing schemes they have sought to gain the economic advantages of his kind of construction without realizing the integrity of the traditional vernacular that his work demonstrates. But given the unorthodox nature of his practice, the unimaginative and elephantine bureaucracy has yet to accept Baker's ideology. Recent work in his home state does not incorporate any of the principles that he has sought to express in his own buildings.

An acknowledgement of the relevance of his ideas can only come from the government which controls a majority of the biggest projects in the country. Baker's iconoclastic system of practice, if put to widespread use, would threaten the very system that has now begun to recognize it. And yet that recognition has come, however grudgingly, compelled by the failure of the establishment to meet the rapidly increasing demand for shelter. Working within wasteful time-frames and budgets, and with a set of antiquated norms, the government has been unable to provide adequate housing for the millions, and has been compelled to turn to Baker for possible solutions. His response—always sincere—is expressed with accurate passion.

> What we will need most are down-to-earth (rather literally is this case) top-quality administrators of the civil service type. They will have to see to the location and acquisition and distribution of land. They will have to organize the continuous availability of simple local building materials and local transport to get them to the building sites. They will have the organizing of workshops for producing a large and steady flow of the simplest doors and windows, etc. They will have to organize the daily availability of cash to pay for labour and materials on the spot. All this contracting nonsense and only being paid when work has been done to a certain level will not work when

70

we are to involve ordinary people and labourers and craftsman in a tremendous labour-intensive job.[18]

Given Baker's position as an architect with a deep understanding of the needs of the rural poor and given his record of successful experiments in housing, the government has sought his advice on its larger projects. He has recently been nominated to several committees concerned with housing. At various times he has been a member of the governing body of the Housing and Urban Development Corporation (HUDCO) and the National School of Design(NID) at Ahmedabad. He has also been on the panel of the Working Group on Housing of the Planning Commission and on several expert committees at the national and state level. He has been conferred an honour by the Royal University of Netherlands (1981) for outstanding work in the Third World and was awarded the Padma Shree in 1990. The citizenship of India, the only title that Baker has actively sought for forty years, was also granted to him then.

> What I've got left of a working life I'd like to concentrate on mud. Not something rural and folksy but proper decent mud building. It's very difficult to get clients for mud building. When it comes to the poor who've already been living on mud, they know it only for its disadvantages. Their dream is a brick-and-cement home.[19]

Now in his mid-seventies, a time when most people savour the years of retirement and inactivity, Baker is in the most creative stage of his life. He remains interested in the local affairs of his city. In fact few natives of Trivandrum have shown as much concern for their city as Baker has. The concern expresses itself in a variety of ways.

A proposed addition to the local stadium, for instance, would have blocked the existing tree line, cut out distant vistas and contributed to a congestion of municipal services. Even after the project was sanctioned and had received the approval of the city administrators, Baker, along with other activists in the city, waged a relentless campaign against its construction. His prolific drawing ability translated to paper the visual impact of the new stadium on the surroundings; and in a series of meticulously-crafted sketches and newspaper articles the group convinced the public of its potential disadvantages. They gathered enough

71

support for the municipal authorities to propose a radically altered scheme.

It is such situations, and perhaps the nature of Laurie Baker's architectural and social responsibility, and even his quiet rebellion against established norms—that has produced in him an increasing irreverence and cynicism. But it is his gentle humour that helps to reconcile to the situation.

Section II

WORK

"ROLL OUT THE BARREL"

NORTH WALL

WEST WALL

SOUTH WALL

EAST WALL

BAR

TABLES

CEILING VENTS FOR LIGHT...

THE INTERIOR to look like the inside of a barrel.
Semi-circular studding lined with thin jack planks
or with commercial ply (thin). Oiled surface only.
Upholstery in rich deep green. Bar-table tops ditto.
Bars & tables to represent half barrels.
Floor yellow mosaic tile
Lighting — natural & indirect thro raised "flaps" of barrel.

SCALE ½" = 1'

L. W. BAKER ARIBA

Introduction

Four decades of Laurie Baker's architectural practice have produced a quantity and range of building not easy to catalogue under the simple classification of 'Projects'. Much of his earlier work in the Pithoragarh district remains undocumented because of Baker's highly idiosyncratic methods of building. A direct mediation of the design with the mason on the site produced architectural drafting that was also done *in situ*. The architect drew the plan on the ground and the skills of the local masons gave it the third dimension. Apart from sketches of life in the Himalayas, Baker retains no record of the schools, missionary hospitals and churches he designed and built in the seventeen years of his life in Pithoragarh.

It is only after he moved to Trivandrum, in 1963, that Baker has had anything like a conventional architectural practice. And even there, sketching, detailing and drawing are done explicitly only for the purposes of construction, and not out of any desire for publication or architectural record.

Consequently, piecing together a comprehensive record of the private residences, churches, institutions, and housing projects was difficult. Some of the projects had working drawings, others only a sketch for the mason, and yet others just a coloured perspective for the client.

Baker's brick houses, institutions and churches were of such a varied range and type that it was difficult to record them all. And it was physically impossible to document each of Baker's thousand houses. Also, many of the projects were located outside Trivandrum. While the smaller of these remain undocumented, a few of the significant institutional buildings in nearby Vellanad, Kottayam and Tiruvella have been included.

The selection of projects for this section, has been largely subjective, reflecting the range and type of buildings designed and built by the architect. Making a selection from a building record of one thousand

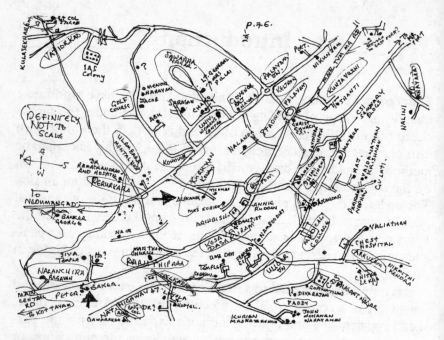

houses and forty institutions is like selecting ten paintings representative of Indian Art from the National Gallery. There are bound to be omissions.

The forty-odd projects presented in this section give an idea of the different characteristics of Baker's architecture through plans, site constructions, building materials, interaction with clients and other details. The architect's intentions, the client's requirements and income, the land's configuration and the subsequent resolution of these concerns into the desired structure are defined in the write-ups that follow.

Mitraniketan
Vellanad, 1970

A familiar concern for the education of local children led to the establishment of an organization called Mitraniketan in Vellanad, a suburban town twelve kilometres from Trivandrum. Being a non-profit group, the organizers wanted to build hostels and training buildings at a low cost and in keeping with the traditional laterite, brick and tile constructions of the area.

The piecemeal development of the seventy-acre site was entrusted to Baker at a time when he had just arrived from the hills of Pithoragarh. In a characteristic fashion, he proposed a series of single-storeyed hostels, training and health buildings, auditorium and staff quarters—not in the manner of an institutional site plan, but as the natural accretion of a village cluster. Baker recalls, 'Materials used were local stone and burnt brick; the general style, a mixture of traditional motifs which dealt with weather conditions; the contemporary use of materials we adapted in structures as simple and direct as possible.'

The buildings were conceived of as independent entities sited on

the boys' hostel

shifting floor levels and approached along footpaths. The architect says, 'This complex is built within an existing coconut palm grove, so the layout was designed to show how even comparatively sizeable buildings could be accommodated without felling any trees.'

The first thing that Baker had to build at Mitraniketan was a house for his own family, as there was a problem of proper accommodation. So, for the three-to-four-month period that he needed to remain on the site to supervise the constructions, Baker designed a round courtyard house for himself. He and an artist friend had gone on ahead of the family and built, in ten days, a structure for less than Rs 2,500 in which they stayed along with their children and Baker's ninety-year-old mother. Baker says, 'It was a sizeable and simple dwelling, circular in form, with practically no internal walls, except for the kitchen and bath—exposed brick supporting a wood-and-thatch roof.' After they

78

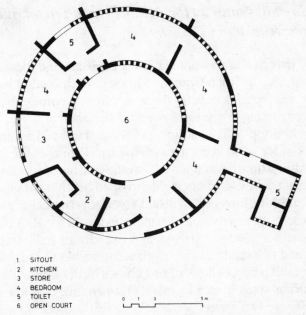

1 SITOUT
2 KITCHEN
3 STORE
4 BEDROOM
5 TOILET
6 OPEN COURT

0 1   3   5 m

left, the director of the organization moved into it and still lives there today.

The special significance of the building is that being near Trivandrum, the design caught the attention of the various guests, workers and officials visiting it, as they felt that this simple wall-less building was an appropriate solution for the hot humid climate of Kerala. Additional proof of its validity was seen in its twenty-odd-year life-span and low-cost. Though by itself this was a small project, for Baker it was to signal the beginning of low-cost housing in the Trivandrum area.

Houses Commissioned by the Archbishop of Trivandrum
Pattom, Trivandrum, 1970

A sizeable part of Kerala's population is Christian and there are many branches of the Christian Church. Although each section has its own principles and special beliefs, there is often a consensus on some ideas—like meeting the housing needs of the poor.

The Archbishop of Trivandrum had decided to build a simple house costing about Rs 3,000 in each parish to provide houses for some poor families. After a time it was realized that the goal had not been achieved and very few parishes had been able to build anything at all. 'There is no longer any thing low cost,' they said. Even government engineers and finance experts concurred that no one could build for Rs 3,000.

Baker, having recently arrived in Trivandrum, took this on as a challenge and offered to prove that it was possible to build for such a sum. In fact, his project—a set of two houses he did for the Archbishop of Trivandrum—was meant to spark of a revolution in low-cost construction. These two houses were Baker's first project in the city. The drawings he prepared for them were done in so simple a manner that even the illiterate mason, or the uninitiated could build without the intervention of an architect or a contractor; instructions alongside had

the two-thousand-rupee house

80

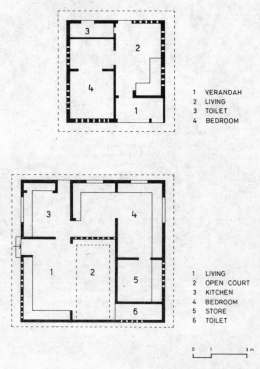

1 VERANDAH
2 LIVING
3 TOILET
4 BEDROOM

1 LIVING
2 OPEN COURT
3 KITCHEN
4 BEDROOM
5 STORE
6 TOILET

the gentle coersion of a how-to manual, instead of the harsh specifications of a blueprint. This has been the mode of planning and operation for almost all his projects. In fact these rough sketches and plans are often redesigned and remodified on the site itself to accommodate for changed or overlooked specifications.

'Excavation should be as shallow as is reasonable—stop digging when solid consistent earth is reached. . . .' instructs Baker.

Built close to each other and in a neighbourhood of cumbersome and expensive buildings, the products had just the right kind of detachment from the locale—there being obvious differences in scale, shape, material and design from anything nearby. Both were made of exposed brick, covered with a wooden structure and Mangalore tile, and exhibited the same concern for privacy, light and ventilation in the use of *jali* walls, courtyard and wall protection.

81

Baker recalls, 'These were small family houses which had cost anything from Rs 1,200 to Rs 3,000; the price including sanitation, minimal electrical facilities, and a kitchen. Obviously such buildings are of necessity small and basic—a compact group of rooms under a minimum roof area. There are very few internal doors, but the arrangement of space allows for privacy between different areas so that differing occupations in the house do not intrude on each other.'

Baker believes that for the greater part of the year extra private living space can be added to such small houses if a small countryard or *anganam* is designed in the centre of the building. 'It can be seen very easily how useful this extra living area is. It is used for drying fish or vegetables. It is used for all sorts of occupations such as basket-weaving or net-making. It is an excellent safe place where children can be left to play. In both houses built-in furniture has been provided by building the granite plinth upto seat-height and these are used as beds and tables.'

Initially, there had been doubt and scepticism about the strength and security that could be provided by the half-brick thick walls and the *jali* windows—but over the next few years several groups did build such houses and they were found acceptable, strong and secure.

Though privately it was accepted that these houses functioned admirably, given the reality of their cost, the project failed to make a lasting and a more widespread impression. It drew sneers from the technocrats and bureaucrats—people in a position to push it into the larger pool of government housing—who felt that the houses were too good for the poor. However, the reason for their discontent, Baker felt, had more to do with the low-profit margins of such projects—this being naturally against the interests of a building establishment that looked to housing for profits rather than the urgency of shelter. When the Chief Engineer of the Public Works Department (PWD) visited the houses and was informed of their cost, he had exclaimed, 'Our establishment fees for such a project would be more than the cost of these houses!'

House for Aniruddhin
Pattam, Trivandrum, 1969

One of Baker's earliest houses, the Aniruddhin residence, presages the simplicity that characterizes his low-cost houses for the Archbishop (p.80). The cost of this project was approximately Rs 20,000. The tile roof sloping inwards to a court, the continuous walls of brick-screen and simple wood-shuttered windows are the most direct expression of Baker's approach to building.

Located on a small plot and set back to save the coconut trees, the external volume of the house has a stark frankness in its inarticulation. The windows are set symmetrically in the wall at regular intervals; the entrance is a door punched into the brick. Inside the house, the same simplicity is reflected in a plan that has virtually no spatial differentiation. The court forms the centre and the rooms connect along it.

Yet, in this simplification is Baker's most radical departure from convention. The house has none of the specific design inputs that would make it particular to the Aniruddhin family. It is a concept for living

the Aniruddhin house

brick screens of the arched court

the window

GROUND FLOOR PLAN

1 MULTIPURPOSE ROOM
2 ROOM
3 KITCHEN
4 VERANDAH
5 COURT

0 1   3 m

realized in its purity. The universal courtyard plan adjusts to the needs of any family. A sweeping arch unites the living area with the court. The rooms around the court are provided the privacy of the brick-screen. The shuttered windows keep the interiors cool on hot afternoons; and when open, they work with the court to draw in air during the humid monsoon months.

'I think it was the first house in Trivandrum of any size to have a preponderance of *jalis* instead of ordinary windows,' says Baker.

85

House for E. Namboodripad
Ulloor, Trivandrum, 1973

On this site enclosed with coconut palms, and steeply sloping to a small stream, Baker proposed a brick tower. 'The length of wall enclosing a given area is shorter when the shape is circular,' says Baker.

The plan develops out of two intersecting circles—the larger drum housing the living and dining rooms on the ground floor and the bedrooms above, the smaller becoming a stair tower. The slope of the stair slab is truthfully expressed in the curve of the circular wall. Pivoted windows and doors, made of simple wooden shutters, are built without frames directly into the jambs. Extensive use of the brick *jali* in exposed

Baker's first sketch of the house

the house under construction

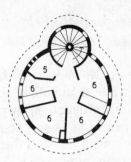

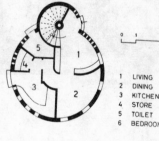

1	LIVING
2	DINING
3	KITCHEN
4	STORE
5	TOILET
6	BEDROOM

brickwork, in areas that require no permanent weather barrier, helped reduce the cost further. The bedrooms upstairs also incorporate some of Baker's ideas of inbuilt furniture, where space for four beds is provided by creating a system of bunks within the wall dividing the circle.

'Everyone found it difficult to believe you could have such a large house with all the plumbing, lighting and built-in furniture for Rs 10,000; but it really was done within that figure. Engineers are convinced I must have skimped on steel or cement, and frequently still inspect it for cracks. But it remains as neat and solid and safe as ever, and they are not very pleased with Mr Namboodripad or myself, because the house refuses to deteriorate or collapse,' says Baker.

House for Nalini Nayak
Anayara, Trivandrum, 1989

Like the Namboodripad house (p.86), the house for Nalini Nayak is a tower house. But unlike the previous house, where site and finance set the vertical direction, the plan adapts a generous sprawling ground floor to a pentagonal tower above.

The main house is formed by a simple three-floor stacking of the pentagon on nine-inch-thick brick walls; internally each floor divides into the bedroom, bath and landing. The additional segment on the ground, forming the living/dining and kitchen, is structured with bays of

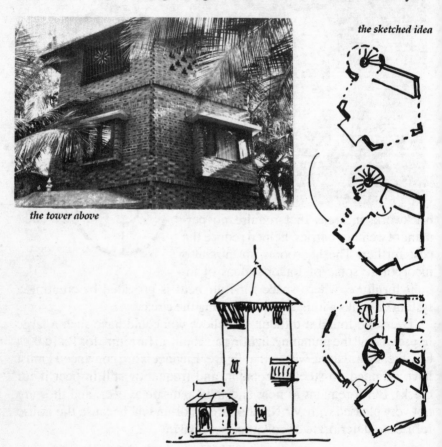

the sketched idea

the tower above

88

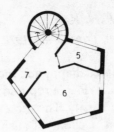

FIRST FLOOR PLAN

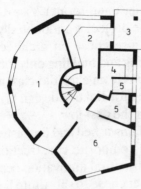

GROUND FLOOR PLAN

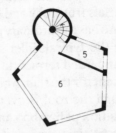

SECOND FLOOR PLAN

1	LIVING	5	TOILET
2	KITCHEN	6	BEDROOM
3	WORK AREA	7	UTILITY
4	STORE		

half-brick thickness, alternating wall and window, wall and door.... The thicker wall was felt unnecessary in a part of the house rising only a single floor. The stair occupies the pivotal position at the centre and fuses with the pentagon above.

Nalini Nayak, a social worker, uses the house for meetings of basket-weavers and fisherwomen, and for training of home nurses. This requires the rooms to function as classrooms in the day and as dormitories at night. In-built furniture of brick, surfaced with terracotta tile serve as sofa and bed; frameless pivot windows have been used, with the protecting grille itself serving as the pivot.

the entrance door

89

House for K.N. Raj
Kumarapuram, Trivandrum, 1970

An 'appreciated, happy and successful home' is how Baker describes his house for K.N. Raj, a reputed economist and former Vice-Chancellor of Delhi University. The success of the project is undoubtedly linked to the fact that a client of such eminence chose an architect with an infamous reputation of low-cost housing and building only for the poor.

Being one of his earliest commissions from a middle-class client, this house was an important testing ground for Baker's design principles of using materials truthfully and keeping the cost low.

The house has the ordinary finish of unwashed and unplastered brick, supporting the typical 'filler-slab'—a composite construction of concrete and discarded terracotta tiles. Structural innovation occurs in the reinforcement for the slab, where Baker chose to substitute bamboo for steel. Though the roof is over twenty years old, Baker maintains that the combination of bamboo and concrete is not appropriate as the two have different time periods for ageing. Yet, symbolically, the house became for Baker a significant extension of his 'low-cost' image to the

the Raj house

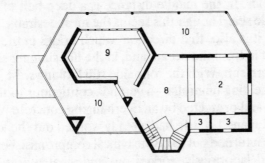

TOP FLOOR PLAN

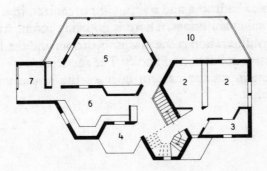

ENTRANCE LEVEL PLAN

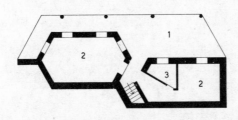

LOWER LEVEL PLAN

1	CAR PORT
2	BEDROOM
3	TOILET
4	VERANDAH
5	DINING
6	KITCHEN
7	WORK AREA
8	LOBBY
9	LIBRARY
10	SITOUT

91

wealthier clients.

The building, sited on a promontory along a steep slope, faces a wide stretch of paddy fields. In the middle distance is a deep belt of palms and a distantly visible sea. Though this seems the most desirable orientation for the view, it is also that direction which brings in the winds and the rain straight in from the ocean, and, in the hot summer season, the afternoon western sun. With the long side still looking west, Baker proposed a deep shielding umbrella—a veranda contiguous to the full length of the house and protected by an overhanging concrete plane.

Baker says, 'Dr Raj and his wife had already worked out the kind of plan they wanted, so it turned out to be the typical compromise between what the clients had laboriously worked out and what the architect would have done had he come in at first....' A low hexagonal entrance brings the visitor into the middle level of a three-storeyed volume. Here the dining room, guest bedroom and a sitout are organized in a series of severe and unequal chamferings. There is no living room. And, up above, in a similar configuration is the master bedroom and the library housing Raj's extensive collection of books. The service areas—stairs, kitchen, toilets—remain on the eastern edge of the house and are retained against the hill.

House for T.N. Krishnan
Kumarapuram, Trivandrum, 1971

Stepped and staggered floors is a feature of virtually every house built on the Kumarapuram hill overlooking the sea. Yet, in each case, peculiar site characteristics and specific family requirements alter the idea into individual compositions—where the Vaidyanathan house incorporates a mango tree within its bounds, the Gulhati residence reconciles the slope within a single space, the Raj house (p.90) makes a feature of the front veranda. In each case the integrity of the house is maintained within a compact volume.

At the Krishnan residence the site is so steeply sloping that Baker chooses to break free of the single mass altogether, splitting the house into a series of volumes stepped one above the other. The site has a fine view of the paddy fields outside, and so the introverted court, which is effectively used in the denser urban settings of the city, is abandoned. An external orientation becomes preferable. The extreme drop of the slope makes it possible for all the rooms to look out over the roofs of the lower rooms.

the rough idea of the house

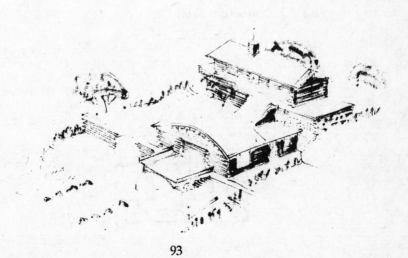

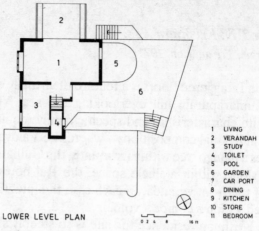

LOWER LEVEL PLAN

0 2 4 8   16 ft

1   LIVING
2   VERANDAH
3   STUDY
4   TOILET
5   POOL
6   GARDEN
7   CAR PORT
8   DINING
9   KITCHEN
10 STORE
11 BEDROOM

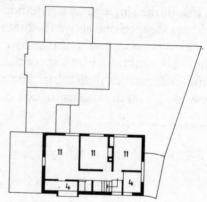

UPPER LEVEL PLAN

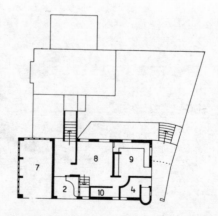

MIDDLE LEVEL PLAN

The house has the appearance of three single-storeyed houses, one below the other, interconnected by roofs and verandas. The middle floor, approached from the top of the hill, houses the public spaces of the house—living, dining, kitchen and car port, with two bedrooms above—while the more private bedroom, den and balcony, slide down to the respective contours below.

Baker explains, 'The family's living and entertainment is in rooms along a continual flight of steps, perched out over the valley and extending onto a wide open balcony precariously holding its own.'

House for Dr P.K. Panikar
Kumarapuram, Trivandrum, 1974

On the other side of the Kumarapuram hill, along a slope of a steepness similar to the Krishnan plot, is one of Baker's earliest houses built for P.K. Panikar, the then Director of the Centre for Development Studies. The approximate cost of this project was Rs 25,000.

Unlike the violent stepping of the Krishnan residence (p.93), the Panikar residence has a quieter, more moderate configuration. Following the shape of the curving contours, the house sits as a single volume directly above a deep depression made by a monsoon stream.

curved fish-tile roof

*the exaggerated roundness
of the house*

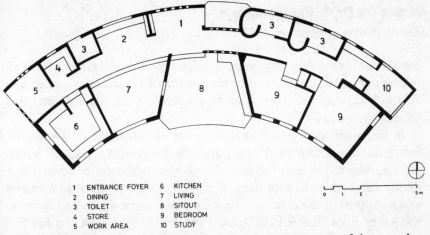

1	ENTRANCE FOYER	6	KITCHEN
2	DINING	7	LIVING
3	TOILET	8	SITOUT
4	STORE	9	BEDROOM
5	WORK AREA	10	STUDY

Baker says, 'This was a difficult house to build because of the terrain, as well as the exaggerated roundness of the slope. And we didn't want to cut too deeply into the hill and prevent cross-ventilation.'

The site was prepared with a plinth of random rubble masonry enclosed by a dry stone retaining wall in the rear. Approaching on a steep decent from the upper road, the visitor enters the living area located centrally in the curving mass and opening into a deep veranda overlooking the hill. The dining and kitchen form one end of the curve, the bedrooms and study the other. Along the walls Baker set up breezeways using the brick *jali*, which also brought a gentler, perpetually altering light to the curved walls.

An overhanging roof of a wide girth and continuous eaves protect the windows, shielding them from the sun and rain. To avoid cracks due to possible sliding and settling, Baker uses the old-fashioned fish-tile roof laid on wooden rafters—the ordinary flat (Mangalore) tile being incapable of taking the curve.

'This is a good example of the fact that the lighter and "less solid" a building is, the stronger it is. The Japanese understood and exploited this principle—but we have never believed it,' Baker explains.

97

House for Dr A. Vaidyanathan
Kumarapuram, Trivandrum, 1972

Two of Baker's more successful circular houses are the ones for T.C.
Alexander (p.101), sited on the gentle slope of Vikramapuram hill, and
A. Vaidyanathan in Kumarapuram, overlooking the paddy fields and
the distant sea.

In the Vaidyanathan house the rooms are arranged in a wide arc
facing the sea. The plan orients outwards in a double semicircle which
incorporates all the major spaces of the house on the upper floor: living,
dining and bedroom, with the semicircle ending in a study at one end
and a car port in the other. A staircase at the entrance travels down to
the lower floor that is built against the retaining wall of the hill and
houses two additional bedrooms and a study. However, the brick walls
of these rooms are separated from the inner stone retaining wall by a

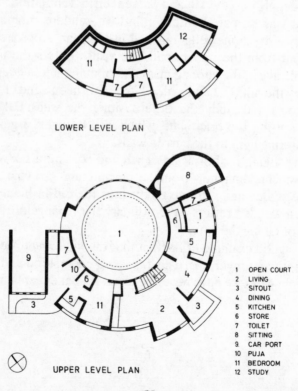

LOWER LEVEL PLAN

UPPER LEVEL PLAN

1	OPEN COURT
2	LIVING
3	SITOUT
4	DINING
5	KITCHEN
6	STORE
7	TOILET
8	SITTING
9	CAR PORT
10	PUJA
11	BEDROOM
12	STUDY

98

around the circle of brick....

through the door....

and into the court

small air space, setting up an effective termite and moisture barrier.

A significant architectural feature of the Vaidyanathan House is an open-to-sky circular court, completing the inner wall of the house in a pattern of staggered brick and becoming the home of an ancient mango tree. Surprisingly, the entrance door is located on the side at the meeting point of the house and court wall—and not on an axial approach as may be expected.

In a finely orchestrated sequence of space the visitor walks across an undefined garden approach, around the circle of brick, into its enclosing court and into the house. Once inside, the focus shifts away from the centre, the concentricity of the circle, to the outward curving walls and the paddy fields beyond.

It is in situations such as these, where an old tree and an awkward slope are reconciled in a composite solution, that Baker's work achieves a sort of earthy on-site lyricism. The physical conditions of the site and their architectural resolution make the visitor aware not of their awkwardness but of the house's naturalness in accommodating them.

brickwork detail

House for T.C. Alexander
Vikramapuram Hill, Trivandrum, 1982

Here again, the circle is used to create an outward and inward orientation. This house costing approximately Rs 75,000 was designed for T.C. Alexander, a retired audit executive.

Baker recalls how the plan for this house was selected, 'I regarded

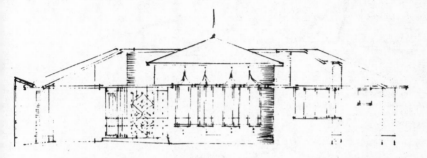

boundary wall and roofscape

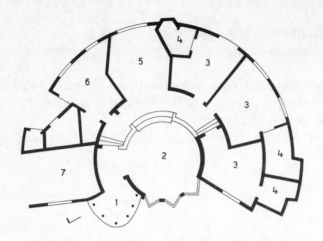

1 ENTRANCE PORCH	5 DINING
2 LIVING	6 KITCHEN
3 BEDROOM	7 CAR PORT
4 TOILET	

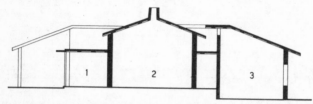

SECTION

raised podium of the living room

entrance porch

the Alexanders as good, social, respectable people who would want a good, social, respectable house. As usual I gave them such a plan and then one or two others—not so solid and respectable. So it was a very happy surprise when they chose the outrageous circular plan!'

On a rectangular plot, the house is formed of a series of concentric circles. Three bedrooms and the dining wall occur along the outer edge of the circle, splaying towards the garden, with the living room as the centre. The guest room is again raised, set askew and, even without a door, the room has a sense of privacy. The Alexanders are apologetic about the absence of the door, 'Mr Baker has promised to put it in one of these days....'

However, the central focus of the house is the living room—a raised circular drum of whitewashed brick, roofed by a hexagonal pyramid and open at the centre with a skylight. The unusual section of the house cleanly separates the central living room from the outer bedrooms. The space in between serves as circulation, its lowered soffit allowing the hot air to ventilate out of the roof. In virtually all his buildings Baker splits the roof with 'a witches cap' so as to set up continuous breezeways. So his buildings rarely require artificial airconditioning.

The changing roof line of the Alexander house adds a spatial complexity to the interior, where the changing height of the volume establishes the relative importance of the rooms. Moreover, this variation is repeated with the floor, which follows the slope of the site, raising the living room on to a podium and, consequently, dropping the corridor and bedrooms around it. The symmetrical relationship between the living and dining areas, the changing levels and the three bay windows also set up an unusual axiality in an otherwise informal plan.

The circular plan has the added advantage of stiffening the wall with less material. Consequently, the external load-bearing walls are nine inches thick while the internal partitions only a single-brick thick. Contained within the latticed brick boundary wall is a garden and an extensive collection of exotic plants.

House for P.J. Thomas
Kuravankonam, Trivandrum, 1972

Another of Baker's very early houses, whose chief distinction is an unusual Y-shaped plan, is located on a difficult sloped site. A low porch in the entrance arm of the Y, propels the visitor into an enormous space made all the more cavernous by a series of pointed arches along its side walls. It is uncertain as to why such a monumental motif is used in a house whose general disposition is towards a gentler setting along the

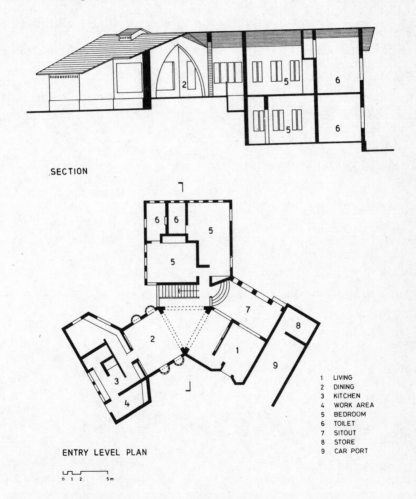

SECTION

ENTRY LEVEL PLAN

0 1 2   5 m

1   LIVING
2   DINING
3   KITCHEN
4   WORK AREA
5   BEDROOM
6   TOILET
7   SITOUT
8   STORE
9   CAR PORT

105

contours. Perhaps a degree of contrast is suggested by the startling juxtaposition. This space forms the main living room of the house with an adjoining dining and kitchen area. From here the bedrooms step down across the arms, overlooking deep columned verandas oriented towards the rear garden. A Mangalore tile roof with deep eaves shades a house built entirely of exposed brick—whitewashed and playing against the dark red-oxide of the floors.

The total cost of this project was approximately Rs 60,000.

House for Lt. Gen. S. Pillai
Jawahar Nagar, Trivandrum, 1971

The Pillais belong to the Nair sect of Kerala, which has evolved a lifestyle so distinctive that it has left a permanent impression on the state's domestic architecture. Living together as a joint family, the Nairs reside in introverted residences organized around a central courtyard. But as individual families grow they also require the privacy of a nuclear set up. The court allows rooms to grow of it, expanding and multiplying with the changing needs, and also, if necessary, becoming private houses.

Pillai's house was designed to accommodate two families. Baker's

entrance veranda

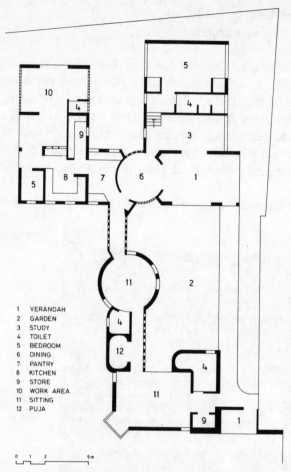

1   VERANDAH
2   GARDEN
3   STUDY
4   TOILET
5   BEDROOM
6   DINING
7   PANTRY
8   KITCHEN
9   STORE
10 WORK AREA
11 SITTING
12 PUJA

0   1   2   5m

solution—in a modified version of the traditional Nair plan—is two houses wrapped around a common interior garden, so that whenever either of the families is temporarily in residence, the house and its 'spread-out-ness' accommodates them easily.

Comparing the house with that of his own Baker says, 'I think these stretched houses, like the Pillai's and the Hamlet, are from a housewife's point of view a lot of work, but from the point of view of the various sections of family life—cooking, wild children, old reminiscers, they are very useful and acceptable. Also when non-family visitors invade, they need not "suffer" family sessions and events, but can have a measure of freedom and privacy.'

The view from the road is of an ordinary single-storey bungalow, set conventionally against a lawn in front of the house. The entrance door appears under a small veranda. When open it reveals not the living room but the interior garden, and so acts as a mediator between two uncovered spaces.

From here, the house moves in a single file, slowly unravelling as it circles the garden. One walks through spaces that have no certain bounds, but in their contraction and expansion, and their exposure and seclusion is the suggestion of how they may be used. Labelling and assigning functions to them seems redundant, for the uses they are put to change constantly. The larger area near the entrance becomes a sitting room, and the one nearer the kitchen a dining room. A bed finds its way to an unused corner, a circular niche in the latticed brick wall acquires a study table and chair. Half-brick thick walls move in spiralling and circular patterns to give additional support to their leanness, and are made even lighter by a fretwork of openings. The changing rhythms of the day, light and shadow are recorded in the shifts that occur in the plan and in a concrete roof of equal exuberance.

bay window

109

House for R. Narayanan
Golf Links, Trivandrum, 1972–73

The house, centred around a mango-shaped countryard, was built for
R. Narayanan, a senior Indian Administrative Service(IAS) officer and
his wife Geeta, an accomplished Bharatanatyam dancer. The house
reflects the graceful movement of this classical dance form as it has been
designed in a curving spiral, around a coconut tree.

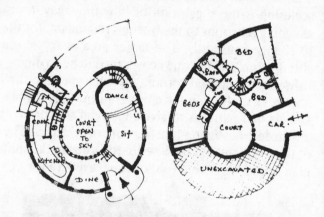

wooden doors of the ancestral home transformed into windows

The plan provides for the diverse requirements of privacy for the family and performing areas for the dance practice. The upper floor, or rather, the upper end of the spiral, includes all the functions of dining, sitting and performance in one curving sweep of space—an idea that is carried through, even in the random placement and size of the windows on the exterior wall. The three bedrooms at the lower end, approached along the perforated court wall, disappear into the ground.

Baker says, 'The house very closely fitted its owners; they had terrific music and dance sessions. Geeta's family and friends are very inclined towards classical music, and a near neighbour is a famous veena player. The house contained these intense and intimate musical sessions well.'

A unique feature is the inclusion of a number of wooden remnants salvaged from an ancestral home which had been pulled down. The boundary wall incorporated an antique gateway; the main entrance of the house is a porch of massive columns, heavily bracketed. 'Door frames were too small to be re-used as doors, so they were re-shaped for windows,' explains the architect, 'No attempt was made at any sort of reconstruction or reproduction of an old type house. We merely made use of the timber to fit in with the new plan and new needs.'

spiralling walls of the court

111

House for Leela Menon
Golf Links, Trivandrum, 1973–74

'Mrs Menon was a widow, and she also had a very ancient mother, bedridden, still with her. She wanted part of her house for a couple in residence who could keep an eye on her mother when she went out visiting and touring. The couple had to be independent but within hearing—and some seeing—distance.' This is how Baker understood the needs of the client.

The house came together as a result of this multifaceted requirement, in an inventive informal pattern. The main approach leads to a sitting room with an adjoining kitchen and a dining area; the bedroom is separate but within the hearing range along with a separate unit for the couple.

Baker adopts these needs to the irregular plot with a variety of interconnected, but geometrically uncertain, shapes. The splaying of walls and the introduction of the toilet to divide space achieves the privacy necessary within the same space. The concrete roof is itself asymmetrical and incorporates pieces of woodwork salvaged from an

Leela Menon's house

112

...he asymmetrical concrete roof

UND FLOOR PLAN

NTRANCE PORCH	5	BEDROOM
IVING	6	TOILET
ITCHEN	7	CAR PORT
INING	8	SITTING

113

old house. Other discarded pieces are resurrected within new frames to form the traditional *jali* windows above the doors and at roof level. Formed of three rough pyramids, the concrete cover is a composition of skylights and water tanks.

salvaged woodwork in the door

House for P. Ramachandran
Puttakyzhy, Trivandrum, 1975–76

Clients are often hesitant to try innovative designs or implement untried concepts on their own buildings. But Ramachandran was not only eager to use innovations but showed great satisfaction in their outcome. This, perhaps, was because the client himself had a knowledge of engineering, he being a senior Civil Engineer of the Posts and Telegraph Department.

The most innovative feature of this project is Baker's skilful application of geometry. The house begins as a straightforward rectilinear volume, sitting snugly on a heavily wooded site. Organized in this compact alignment, the main rooms assert their own individual identity by breaking out of the preset bounds. The corner sitting room springs a set of bay windows; the guest room extends into the rear garden; and the main entrance and car porch make a similar gesture in the front. The need for ventilation in tropical Kerala makes a double exposure mandatory for every room.

In a Baker house there is rarely, if ever, the need for formal circulation, like enclosed corridors. Access to bedrooms is through the family

the house on a heavily wooded site (inset: *bay window*)

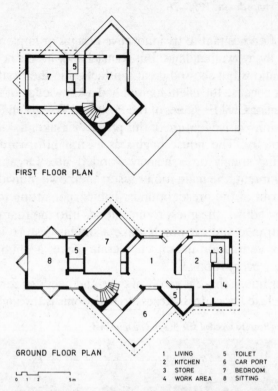

FIRST FLOOR PLAN

GROUND FLOOR PLAN

0 1 2   5m

1	LIVING	5	TOILET
2	KITCHEN	6	CAR PORT
3	STORE	7	BEDROOM
4	WORK AREA	8	SITTING

rooms of the house, and the stairs are so worked that they land directly into the upper bedrooms—without corridors or peripheral walkways.

Modest detailing, effectively harnessed, makes the simple volume of a room appear different from others. The bay windows in the living room are more than mere decorative niches—the shutters, on a cantilevered slab, open fully to expose the room to the outside on three sides. Lattice brick walls are used in rooms requiring no permanent closure.

The lesser details of wiring and lighting fixtures have been planned with careful deliberation of design and economy. Baker adds, 'I use waste wood for these combinations of light and electrical sockets; the drops (wires) are concealed behind the wood and only the carved bracket appears against the brick wall. Some are quite elaborate with rotating arms so you can swing the light where you need it.'

116

House for Ravindranath
Gourishapattom, Trivandrum, 1975

One of Baker's smaller projects, the house for the Ravindranaths, like that of several others, springs from severe site limitations: an awkward slope, a small plot with too many trees on it which needed to be accommodated in the design.

The Ravindranath house is unique in Baker's minimization of building material and elimination of all inessential elements. The primary motive for simplification is, naturally, the reduction of cost. Particularly striking features are: the floor slab set flush with the outer wall and cantilevered as a protection for the windows, the wall at the corners where the intersecting brick is left uncut, and the absence of lintels for all openings.

The plan is also the result of simply articulated spatial compression. The shape is a stretched hexagon of two storeys—the lower floor houses a family room and a kitchen, and it is connected by a hidden corner staircase, to a bedroom and bath above.

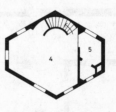

FIRST FLOOR PLAN

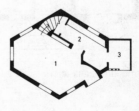

GROUND FLOOR PLAN

0 1   3m

1	LIVING
2	KITCHEN
3	YARD
4	BEDROOM
5	TOILET

117

House for Abu Abraham
Kowdiar, Trivandrum, 1989

Situated in an old neighbourhood of Trivandrum the house of cartoonist and columnist, Abu Abraham, is built on a site having two gnarled trees. The other houses nearby—some modern, some not so successful imitations of the vernacular—lend a kind of dubious lineage to the area. In their midst, this house designed by Baker sits with a quiet assurance. Its rectilinear plan projects an entrance portico to the outside, but orients the main volume to the internal focus of a courtyard. Behind the portico, the formal and informal living areas meet through a series of arched openings; brick-work patterns and rat-trap bonding walls are left exposed. Random rubble stone foundations are allowed to rise and form an outer shell for the ground floor of the house.

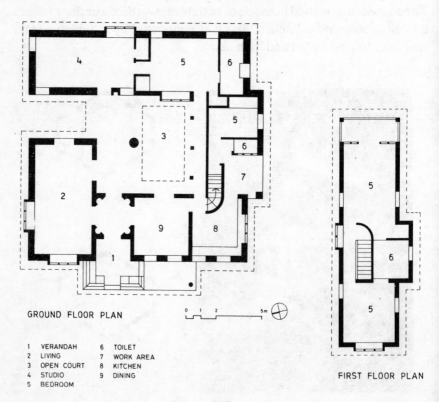

GROUND FLOOR PLAN

1	VERANDAH	6	TOILET
2	LIVING	7	WORK AREA
3	OPEN COURT	8	KITCHEN
4	STUDIO	9	DINING
5	BEDROOM		

FIRST FLOOR PLAN

118

courtyard details

In the relative seclusion of the rear lies Abu's workroom, beyond the relieved end of the linear space, under a hipped roof ventilated at the ridge. There are windows on all sides above the sight line, a requirement for adequate, yet changing light in a studio; the bedroom overlooks a pond in the court and connects across an open arcade to the front of the house. The kitchen and the servants room, forming a shuttered edge to the court, also contain a staircase to the two upper bedrooms and a roof garden.

House for Varghese Jacob
Kottayam, 1976

The traditional courtyard organization of the Kerala house, which brings several extended families to a central community focus, is here used paradoxically, to disperse functions within the same plan. Generated by a series of circles eccentric to a central court, the public and private faces of the house divide like the wedge-shaped pieces of a common pie.

The plan sets up an axiality between the formal spaces of the building: the front office aligning with the court, and the court with the living

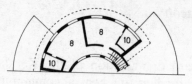

FIRST FLOOR PLAN

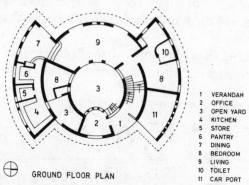

GROUND FLOOR PLAN

1 VERANDAH
2 OFFICE
3 OPEN YARD
4 KITCHEN
5 STORE
6 PANTRY
7 DINING
8 BEDROOM
9 LIVING
10 TOILET
11 CAR PORT

room beyond. But with the circles making such a pervasive presence the axis becomes secondary and unrealized.

Movement through the house is seen in the nature of a spiralling journey. An entrance along a side veranda opens to the circulation along the wall of the courtyard, a split staircase takes one down with the slope of the land into a drawing room that opens onto the rear garden. A great band of doors and windows set up an atmosphere of an open pavilion and allow cross currents into the centre court. The outer circle incorporates the dining, kitchen, storage and servant's room, and ends in a service court. Having come a full circle the door leading out emerges by the front office.

The concept of using a circle to organize home is a curious one, but Baker's sensitivity to the client's needs and to the natural layout of the site allows for a restful adjustment and a sensuous tactility. This makes the geometry appear most suited for the plan. The elimination of needless circulation and the feeling of openness and intimacy are attributes of a design attitude that readily absorbs the monumental shape and, equally willingly, alters it.

House for K.V. George
Karakullam, Trivandrum, 1987

This house, built across a bridge and isolated from the road by a palm grove and a meandering stream, is as unusual in its setting as it is for the details of its construction. For, on the quiet bank, under the darkness of the trees, there reflects in the still waters a house that has the appearance of a vernacular stage set built in the Baker tradition of exposed brick, incorporating within windows, eaves, roofs and parapets a multitude of crafted carvings.

The house, approached from the side, is organized behind a central living room, two storeys high, with the stairwell curving along its wall. Upper bedrooms also open into its volume but orient outwards to the stream and the landscape in the front.

The owner, a bank manager, with a passion for buying carved wooden antiques—columns, rafters, doors, screens, etc. insisted that Baker make the right architectural setting for his collection. Initially this seemed an interesting challenge and space was left along walls, niches were left incomplete, openings unfilled so as to transform the burgeon-

the house across the bridge

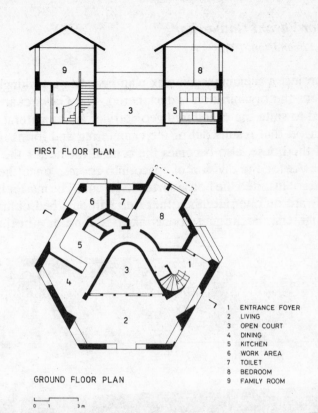

FIRST FLOOR PLAN

GROUND FLOOR PLAN

1 ENTRANCE FOYER
2 LIVING
3 OPEN COURT
4 DINING
5 KITCHEN
6 WORK AREA
7 TOILET
8 BEDROOM
9 FAMILY ROOM

0 1   3 m

ing antiques into a more useful contemporary purpose. 'But,' says Baker, 'throughout the course of building the owner could not stop buying more and more. Everyday a few more pieces would arrive in a truck, and he would insist we use them somewhere. It was all fun in the beginning, but while I was trying to finish the work, he was still furiously buying up old pieces—until finally it began to look like the junk shop where these items had come from.'

House for Vasant Gawarekar
Manvila, Trivandrum, 1982

In this project a seemingly complex plan becomes a strikingly simple one, when the organization is deciphered. The Gawarekar house is organized to suite the chamfered geometry of an equilateral triangle. The hexagon that results out of the chamfering and forms the outer shape of the house, also becomes the central theme for the internal structure. As for the division of space into rooms, 'once the central courtyard got inserted the house sorted itself out'. The master bedroom and study are on one side; the other side harbours bedrooms for the three daughters; and the guest rooms take position along the third edge.

Though the family needs are admirably met, the equality of the triangle and its dominating shape, made it difficult to set up heirarchical relationships of space and scale between the rooms, between the front and the back, and between the outside and the inside—factors that occur more naturally in Baker's other, less geometrically-ordered houses. The final effect is of a severe shape being adjusted to personal requirement.

skylights inside

skylights out

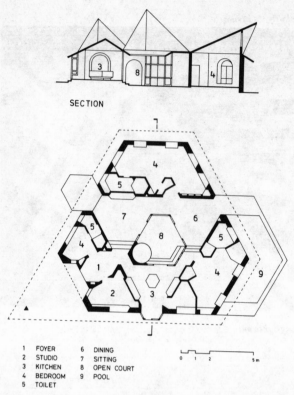

SECTION

1	FOYER	6	DINING
2	STUDIO	7	SITTING
3	KITCHEN	8	OPEN COURT
4	BEDROOM	9	POOL
5	TOILET		

0 1 2   5 m

The house is unusual in another way. The external shell of stone harbours internal divisions of exposed brick. Details of living are fashioned in and around structural piers in a single-brick thickness, setting up a contrasting randomness to the rigorous plan. Rubble masonry walls along with the internal brick piers support a folded slab roof. Skylights within the roof allow diffused light into rooms and, in conjunction with the court, act to draw in the breeze.

'I think a house is not really well designed if it has to rely on fans and air-conditioners; so to make sure this complicated cluster of triangles got well ventilated I added these irregular pyramids with one side open to funnel in the sea breezes,' says Baker.

House for Beena Sarasan
Kowdiar, Trivandrum, 1989

Reduced building costs often allow clients to build more than they need. Though this is certainly creditable, the combination of eccentricity of the client and ideas on cost reduction are tricky to handle. This is best illustrated by a recent house Baker did for Beena Sarasan, an income-tax officer.

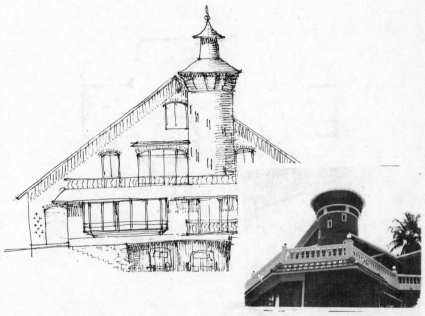

The house is located in the older, more posh, neighbourhood of Trivandrum, midway between the Tennis Club and the Golf Course. The plan makes the best use of a steeply sloping trapezoid.

The placement of the puja room has played an important part in determining the building section, and this is evident in the prominence and isolation given to the tower room and the study. The secondary spaces of day-to-day living are fitted into a convenient A-frame, with a bridged courtyard at the centre.

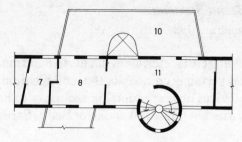

FIRST FLOOR PLAN

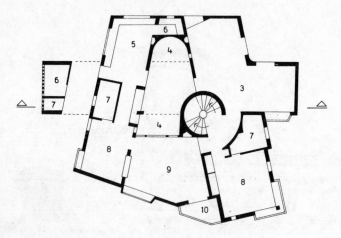

GROUND FLOOR PLAN

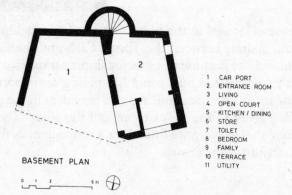

BASEMENT PLAN

1 CAR PORT
2 ENTRANCE ROOM
3 LIVING
4 OPEN COURT
5 KITCHEN / DINING
6 STORE
7 TOILET
8 BEDROOM
9 FAMILY
10 TERRACE
11 UTILITY

0 1 2   5 ft

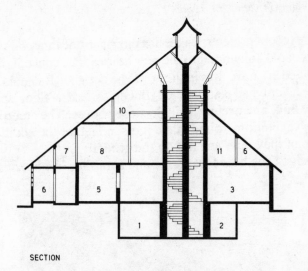

SECTION

The basement approach takes the visitor through an entrance room, up a circular stair into the inhabited domain: the family rooms in front, and the formal drawing and dining rooms in the rear. Further up, the stair takes one into realms of increasing privacy—past an elongated library, through a gallery and study floor, into a circular lighthouse-like room partially open to sky. This is the house of worship.

Architecturally, the uniqueness is found not just in the client's un-usual orientation to worship but also in bringing together a hybrid of building parts: highly polished windows of the Kerala vernacular sit in walls made in typical Baker brick-bonds and topped by white colonial balustrades. Indigenous, low-cost, but classical, the ancestry of the house remains suspect. It is the result of accommodating the peculiar and specific wishes of a client, persistant on the latter's personalized identification. Had not the architect's stamp been evident in its crafting, the house may have easily integrated in any of the city's newer suburbs.

131

House for Anna Mathew
Kuravankonam, Trivandrum, 1986

In his more recent projects, Baker has shown an uncanny ability to adapt fragments of old buildings into the new houses. The concept of retrofitting is applied in a novel way in the house he designed for Anna Mathew. Here, the client had approached Baker for extra floor space to a previously built and occupied single-storey house. The steep contours and heavy vegetation around made it essential that the addition occur on the top of the house and not on the ground.

Baker says, 'The house was large and sprawling but not designed to

front veranda

entrance stair

133

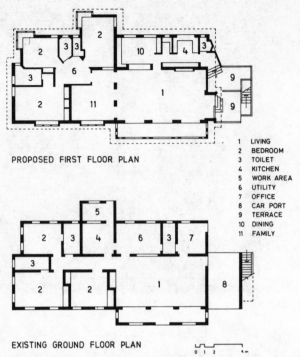

PROPOSED FIRST FLOOR PLAN

1	LIVING
2	BEDROOM
3	TOILET
4	KITCHEN
5	WORK AREA
6	UTILITY
7	OFFICE
8	CAR PORT
9	TERRACE
10	DINING
11	FAMILY

EXISTING GROUND FLOOR PLAN

take a second floor according to the original plan. I tried to make the two halves compatible—visually at least—but the layout was determined by the load-bearing walls below.'

An architectural marriage between such two diametrically opposite halves was naturally a very tricky one. For the one below was heavy and ponderous, designed in the modern way, wasteful of building material, and plastered and painted with all the radiance of emulsion; the other, above, was light and airy separated only by the line of the old parapet, controlling the material in a thin envelope and presenting a simple whitewashed face to the outside.

The difference becomes obvious while approaching the house. The entrance above the existing car port angles a latticed brick wall towards the visitor, but effectively conceals the kitchen door behind corbelled walls. In plan the private areas of the house organize not along a conventional corridor but through a family room.

134

House for K.O. Peter
Nalanchira, Trivandrum, 1988

About the project Baker says, 'I think the Peters' house is one of my more successful "house on house" houses. Not unlike Miss Mathew's, this too was a typical modern house with "sun louvres and fins on the side" with plaster and bright enamel to give the front just that right importance of elevation. The structuring too was cumbersome, relying on an excessive use of concrete for short room spans.'

What made the house a success was perhaps Peter's less demanding area requirement for the upstairs, and his giving the architect a free hand in its manipulation.

house on house

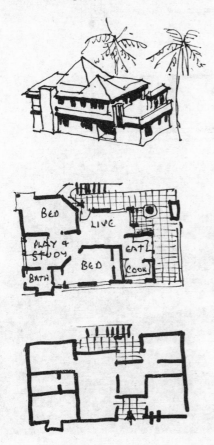

135

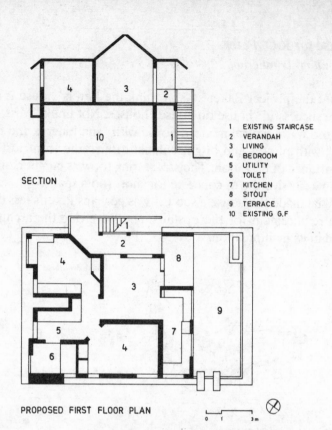

SECTION

1 EXISTING STAIRCASE
2 VERANDAH
3 LIVING
4 BEDROOM
5 UTILITY
6 TOILET
7 KITCHEN
8 SITOUT
9 TERRACE
10 EXISTING G.F

PROPOSED FIRST FLOOR PLAN

0   1   3m

136

The upper house built for Peter's daughter and her husband required the intimate links of a joint family as well as the independence of a nuclear one.

Baker says, 'In this case the younger parents wanted a simpler type of house than the "modern" ground floor. So we built on top of it. Though the same plan was not desired, our only constructional requirement was to build our first storey walls above the ground floor walls.'

The upstairs is approached by an separate stair in the rear, landing into an arched veranda. The living area and kitchen open on to a terrace, while there are two bedrooms at the rear of the house. In the main bedroom the bed is fashioned out of the old concrete water tank, now used for storage. Thin walls of exposed brick are topped by a sloped filler tile slab and contrast radically with the burdened heaviness of the house below. This is certainly another successful aspect of the addition where neither the client nor the architect have felt any aesthetic compulsion to merge the two houses. The upper home different in all respects—texture, design, weight, silhouette and usage—is allowed to appear resting on the lower one with all the material, textural and chromatic reference to bourgeoisie oppulence.

House for S. Valiathan
Pulliyankotta, Trivandrum, 1985–86

Another instance of an architectural modification of a different sort is the house Baker built for S. Valiathan, one of Trivandrum's famous cardiac surgeon, and his wife, a dental surgeon.

The house started its life as a conventional, over-designed, two-storey structure built by the State Housing Board, but was abandoned on the completion of the outer shells, 'without flooring, ceiling or finishes'. The Valiathan's were offered the house in this incomplete state on the condition they finished it themselves with no further responsibility of the Housing Board. Baker was then brought in to perform a kind of architectural surgery.

He says, 'The Valiathan plot was on a corner of the colony overlooking the paddy fields, and in the distance, the sea. So we used the basic plan, but added various other rooms and facilities.' Since the outer shell already existed and the lower floor was occupied by the living, dining and guest bedroom, Baker had to work within the restrictive bounds of the first floor and roof to accommodate a library and study for Valiathan, a dental surgery for his wife and a mediating family room. This was accomplished with the introduction of a mezzanine level. Baker adds, 'We added quite a bit of floor area while having to retain the typical "modern" plan and elevations, with all the proturberances I deplore. It was frustrating trying to build into someone else's work, and I'm afraid the additions and alterations invariably remain secondary to the original plan.'

138

A Residential Cooperative
Vattiyorkavu, Trivandrum, 1983–85

A housing colony was built in Trivandrum for retired officers of the Indian Administrative Service (IAS). Land procured from the government for the co-operative venture was divided into plots, and the owners approached Baker to design the houses. A housing co-operative of several privately-owned plots is not an unusual project for any architect, but the fact that Baker chose to provide individual designs for each client, rather than repeat the same unit, makes for a unique interpretation of the co-operative idea.

*y plan: this shows how the site had already been divided into 2 straight lines of square plots. The variously
d spaces were used to create little open spaces (a variety of them) to avoid the monotony of 2 straight lines of houses.*

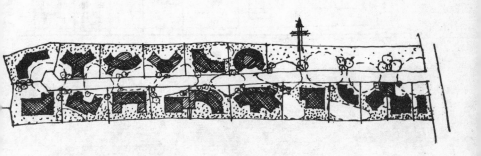

'What I did was talk with the client, ask the family what they wanted, what kind of buildings they would be happy in. If they were fairly orthodox I gave them a straightforward plan. If I thought they were more adventurous then I did an outlandish plan—a round one or a triangular plan. And I presented all three and left it to them to make the choice. If they had individual plots I am sure they would have selected the simple, unimaginative house, but because they were all together in a small colony they all picked the outrageous ones. Now there are circular houses, moon-shaped and heart-shaped houses.... but all in exposed brick.' says Baker.

House for K.J. Mathew
Vattiyorkavu, Trivandrum, 1983–85

Among the houses at Vattiyorkavu this building has both the monumental appeal of an outer street face and the intimacy of a personalized interior. Baker achieved this duality by rigorously working the functions into a predetermined geometry.

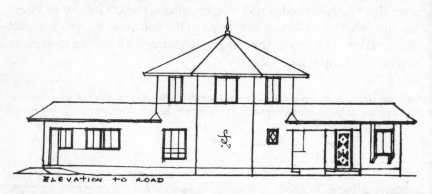

ELEVATION TO ROAD

140

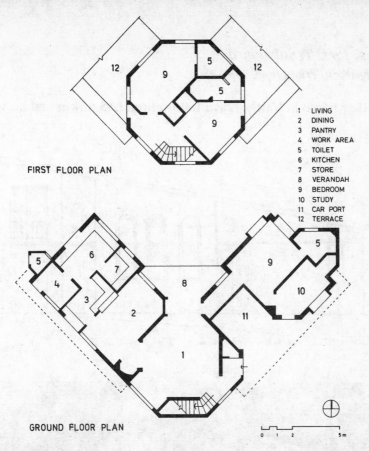

FIRST FLOOR PLAN

1	LIVING
2	DINING
3	PANTRY
4	WORK AREA
5	TOILET
6	KITCHEN
7	STORE
8	VERANDAH
9	BEDROOM
10	STUDY
11	CAR PORT
12	TERRACE

GROUND FLOOR PLAN

The shape of the hexagon is allowed to materialize in the centre of the house and rise above the outer symmetry of the single storey. But inside, the formality of the mass is concealed by Baker's proverbial carving, realigning and adjusting space into bedrooms, storage and toilets. The double wall within the hexagon obscures the entrance and access to a secondary space, and makes for an organization that gives a significant focus to the geometry.

The lower floor of the drum, which houses the drawing room, becomes a meeting point for two households that stretch out as arms from the hexagon, the family areas below and bedrooms above; the adjoining single room and study apartment are occupied by the visiting in-laws. The car port splits this efficiently built apartment from the main house and ensures a certain privacy for both units.

House for C.T. Sukumaran
Vattiyorkavu, Trivandrum, 1983–85

Another house in Vattiyorkavu for a retired IAS officer and his wife,

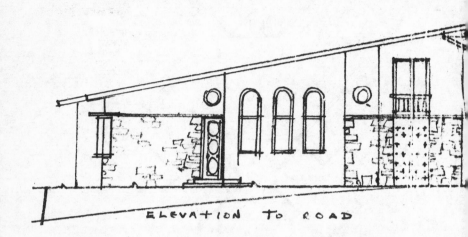

ELEVATION TO ROAD

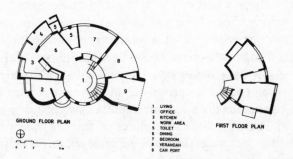

GROUND FLOOR PLAN

FIRST FLOOR PLAN

1 LIVING
2 OFFICE
3 KITCHEN
4 WORK AREA
5 TOILET
6 DINING
7 BEDROOM
8 VERANDAH
9 CAR PORT

who is a dancer, has none of the grace and spiral curves of the original 'dancer' house Baker had done for the Narayanans (p.110). Since the requirement is not determined by space for performance, the house acquires a more conventional disposition—one similar to the numerous round-houses Baker has built.

Yet the purity of the circle is not maintained in this plan, and though the bedrooms are offshoots of the central living room, the circle has neither the axial formality and elevation of the Alexander home (p.101) nor the complementary adjacency of the circular court of the Vaidyanathans(p.98). The living room is merely a convenient appendage of circulation, both on the ground floor as well as above. The lower rooms are entered through the living room, and a staircase within it leads to the bedrooms above. The importance of the circle is further diminished by cutting into it a flat slab serving as a terrace for the upper floor.

The uncertainty in plan carries into the materials; and the house, constructed of brick, has been given a curving face-lift of stone masonry.

There are obviously limits as to how much the questing conscience of an architect can influence a middle-class architectural morality. For clients with dubious but pervasive ideas on aesthetic appeal, Baker's role as a catalyst cannot be comfortable. The application of façade elements on the structurally-restrained building has produced a strangely incongruous vanity.

143

House for P.K. Sivanandan

Vattiyorkavu, Trivandrum, 1983–85

A curious Y-shaped house falls at the end of the street of the Vattiyorkavu colony. The shape has little to do with plot dimension or configuration but arises out of a requirement set by the owner. P.K. Sivanandan, a yoga enthusiast, needed a separate part of the house for his morning activities. Baker says, 'Yoga is a way of life for him and in one upper wing the art is carried out in a room open on three-sides, above the car port, with a large triangular skylight for the 'rising-sun worship'; while study, and other states of mental transformation are practised in the enclosing corners of the same room, two adjacent nooks track the morning and evening sun.'

The arms of the Y-shaped house converge in a two-storeyed hexagon which, like the Mathew house(p.140) up the same street, becomes the main living room. From here the family circulates—to the guest room and the kitchen below, and to the bedrooms and yoga wing above. Again, the hexagon, though central to the circulation of the house, is effectively protected by a double wall that conceals the stairs, storage

yoga room above the car port

144

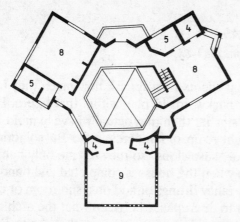

FIRST FLOOR PLAN

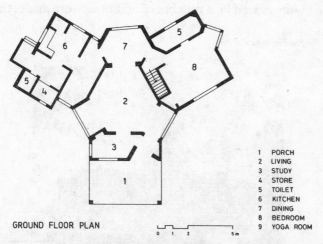

GROUND FLOOR PLAN

1	PORCH
2	LIVING
3	STUDY
4	STORE
5	TOILET
6	KITCHEN
7	DINING
8	BEDROOM
9	YOGA ROOM

0 1 2   5 m

and passages of the house. A skylight splits the filler slab above the hexagon to provide light to the central space.

The adaptability of many such houses to the client's specific needs and requirements makes them unsuitable for occupation by anybody else; and change cannot be accommodated easily. Baker maintains that they are designed with the most democratic of personal choices, by and for the people who see it as their only and lasting architectural commitment.

145

House for T. Sukhman
Vattiyorkavu, Trivandrum, 1983–85

'When I meet potential clients I always ask how much they intend to spend, and then work backwards to plan within that figure. But most people give me a sum smaller than they actually have in mind, which is fair enough. Prices might go up, or I underestimate. But sometimes they are just too cautious or "suspicious" so they tell me only half of what they actually have. So when the house is completed and handed over, they dash out and buy fancy fittings or add on a sun room or car port,' says Baker. This leads to discrepancy between what the architect considers as a completed liveable house and how the owner alters this perception to his own personal taste in the course of his occupation.

An illustration of this is found the Sukhman house, one of Baker's better solutions dramatically altered to utilize the client's real budget. After the family moved in, a number of additions were made, that 'look

the Sukhman house

146

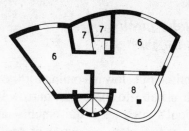

FIRST FLOOR PLAN

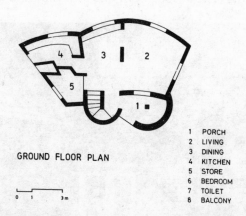

GROUND FLOOR PLAN

1	PORCH
2	LIVING
3	DINING
4	KITCHEN
5	STORE
6	BEDROOM
7	TOILET
8	BALCONY

0   1   3 m

a bit tacked on', though obviously not enough to alter the original plan.

One of the smallest houses in the colony, this was generated from an unusual plan, too compact for the large plot on which it is sited. The quality of tightness was a requirement of the client who was not keen on the sprawling garden house or the traditional courtyard house.

The plan, consequently, reflects a certain spatial proxomity achieved as a result of the miniaturization. On the ground floor, the entry along a curved porch and circular stairwell lands one at the very focus of the convex ground floor wall—living, dining and kitchen, all lying in a simple gesture of physical and visual convenience. Upstairs, a similar show of constriction and eventual release is experienced in the snug landing, opening onto splaying bedrooms and a balcony. Baker's skilful manipulation of the undulating rear is meant to contrast the narrowness of the entrance and the open view of the garden in the rear.

147

House for Lt. Col. John Jacob
Kulasekhanam, Trivandrum, 1988

Funds were not so limited but slow in coming for the Jacob house, built on a long rectangular urban site somewhat narrow in breadth. Baker's resolution of the client's complex requirements and site constraints helped to generate, in the plan, a degree of spatial and elemental playfulness, a characteristic absent in the houses of his less fortunate clients. He says, 'The Jacobs were one of my most helpful and accom-

modating clients. They knew what they wanted, and they knew how to ease it out of me.' The subtle mixing of stone with brick, the overlapping of *jali* walls and window, the minor adjustments in the interior levels may not have been possible if the house had been built with the desperation of shelter. This is not to suggest that the Jacob house is pretentious, but merely that Baker has crafted a degree of personalized articulation into his regularly-used repertoire of architectural details.

The unusual feature of the house is the use of random stone masonry which forms the plinth line in front, rises to sill level in the rear, where the floor line drops and becomes the retaining platform for the garden. It is to this, to the watery landscape so skilfully manoeuvred, that the house is oriented. Windows in bays and clerestories, frame the view out of varying arches on both floors. The dual function of the

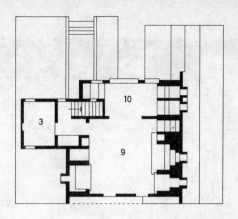

UPPER LEVEL PLAN

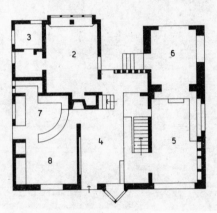

ENTRY LEVEL PLAN

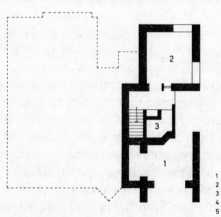

LOWER LEVEL PLAN

1   CAR PORT
2   BEDROOM
3   TOILET
4   ENTRANCE FOYER
5   LIVING
6   COURT
7   KITCHEN
8   DINING
9   CHILDREN'S ROOM
10   SITOUT

0   1   2   5m

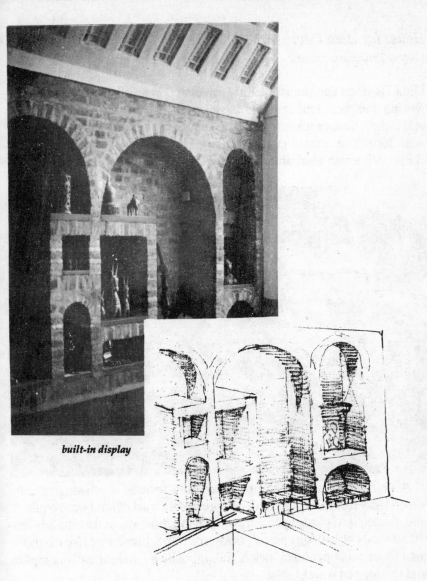

built-in display

operable shutter in the room wall and the arched opening in the outer wall combine to create intermediate verandas and sitouts. The double wall, effectively tuned, controls the light, limiting the glare, and enriching the textures of brick and tile with an even glow.

151

House for Uma Devi
Ulloor, Trivandrum, 1989

Uma Devi, an economist at the University, 'wanted a place to do her writing and meet students and have enough guest space for her sister and father, both of whom spend time with her, and also her female guru next door. The female guru, of course, has twenty-four large wooden chests, Victorian almirahs of all the goods she has renounced.'

A number of university professors had formed a housing society which Uma Devi hastily joined. A large square tract of land was acquired and divided into plots, by the drawing of lots. She was unfortunately left with a 'nasty little boggy place' sticking out from the square like a handle on a saucepan, but which luckily fell opposite a Hindu temple complex and its stepped water tank.

What had become a matter of personal embarassment to Uma Devi was deftly reversed by Baker into a source of genuine pride. If Uma Devi had felt cheated in the land deal, it was her colleagues who felt swindled after the house was built, for few among them could have imagined that the appropriation of muddy, water-logged ground could offer such a

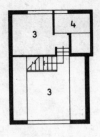

FIRST FLOOR PLAN

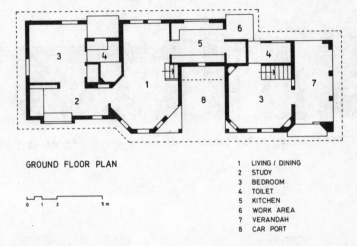

GROUND FLOOR PLAN

0 1 2   5 m

1 LIVING / DINING
2 STUDY
3 BEDROOM
4 TOILET
5 KITCHEN
6 WORK AREA
7 VERANDAH
8 CAR PORT

substantial solution.

The house falls along a narrow strip of land opposite the temple complex and forms a linear volume enclosing the reservoir. The unusual spread of the plan makes the house appear deceptively large but becomes necessary because of the site configuration.

The peculiar limitations of the site are used positively to provide additional exposure to the rooms. The study and living areas are oriented towards the water tank, and large window areas draw the air across its surface cooling the rooms through cross-ventilation.

At the centre the two households come together, sharing a kitchen veranda on the ground, and a common terrace on the roof where skylights are inserted into its folded surface. Brick walls in both the wings are kept entirely exposed both inside and out, while an elaborate system

153

of internal shelving, study tables and seating arrangements is built into the walls.

House for Vinay Kumar
Kunjavuzni, Trivandrum, 1990

Vinay Kumar, an English teacher at Loyola college, had always found
the family house that he inherited a bit too inconvenient and sprawling
with dark and ill-ventilated rooms despite the plan's unusual spread.
The building, designed as a corridor house, had been planned quite
unimaginatively without any consideration for privacy, family living and
differentiation of work areas—the essential characteristics of a home.
While the toilets and stores lined the front street edge, the bedrooms
had no openings on any outside wall, the living room served only to
connect another bedroom, and the study to the corridor. The overall

existing plan

1	LIVING / DINING
2	STUDY
3	BEDROOM
4	TOILET
5	STORE
6	WORK AREA
7	KITCHEN
8	VERANDAH
9	SITTING
10	PANTRY
11	YOGA ROOM
12	DARK ROOM
13	CAR PORT
14	OPEN COURT

EXISTING PLAN

0   1   2   5 m

155

proposed plan

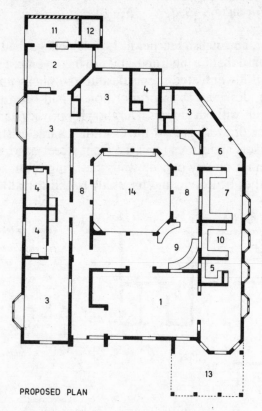

PROPOSED PLAN

plan had all the sensitivity and tenderness of bureaucratic house design.

Faced with this scheme, Baker attempted to achieve a sense of home by redesigning and relocating each room according to its appropriate heirarchy. Bedrooms opened out with bay windows; the services spaces of kitchen–store–servant moved to the far end. Thus the house closed in upon itself around a central court, making the circulating corridor of the previous plan into a useful veranda. These changes, however, were accomplished with minimum demolition and with due regard to the established building bounds.

156

Gate House for P.J. Joseph
Todupuzha, Trivandrum, 1977

A consciousness of security, the need to maintain a public image separate from the private reality became the calling for a guard house gate and garage complex that Baker designed for the former Chief Minister of Kerala, P.J. Joseph.

P.J. Joseph lived in an old family home, designed by his grandfather, for several years before the family had any political aspirations. The family house was not designed 'to cope with the crowds that would descend upon a minister at all hours of the day and night giving little peace and privacy to the family'. The architectural brief given to Baker was deceptively simple—a control point at the boundary of the present house for pedestrian callers, and a waiting area and a garage for the Minister's cars.

Baker's active imagination and his sharp perception understood the nature of his client's demand; his architectural sensitivity created a place

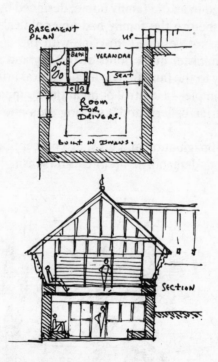

that goes beyond the mere provision of a covered area called for in the brief. Baker's design, always infinitely more conscious of human needs than those of the automobile, proposed a traditional gate complex that incorporated spaces for the security staff and drivers as well as a cover for the Minister's cars.

The building is housed in a thickening of the boundary wall—a wall acquiring space for habitation, a tile roof for protection. The guard house, with built-in platforms, is shielded from view by the perforations of a *jali*; and a driver's room, similarly, with bath and veranda built above

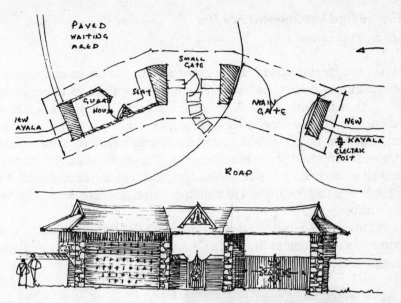

a common meeting room, follow the wooden bracket construction of a traditional house.

The complex makes a spatial statement of the need for security and suggests a place of arrival in a formal sequence to the house.

Centre for Development Studies
Ulloor, Trivandrum, 1971

While the greater part of Baker's professional life has been devoted to the making of houses, he has also dealt with commissions of public and institutional nature. In 1967, when he was asked to design a centre for research in applied economics in Ulloor, a suburb of Trivandrum, Baker expressed his building ideas in one convincing sweep in, what is today, the most important project of his career. The significance of this assignment had less to do with size and budget, than with the idea of exhibiting a range of concepts applied to buildings of varying functions, scale and dimensions.

An area of nine acres accommodates administrative offices, a computer centre, an amphi-theatre, a library, classrooms, housing and other components of an institutional design.

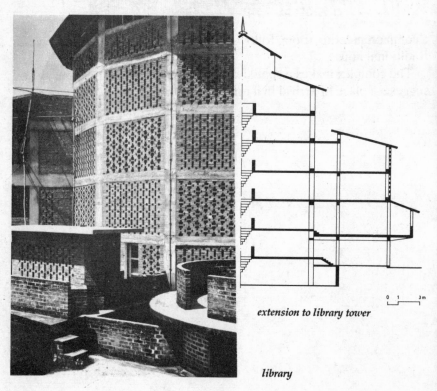

extension to library tower

library

Baker's expertise was required not merely to make this into a cost-effective complex, but to provide a setting with an image consistent with its development-conscious goals. On a hillside, overlooking paddy fields, the site rises in a difficult gradient of rocky soil up to the crest of a hill. Here, at the summit, the library dominates the centre with a seven-storey tower; the administrative offices and classrooms are scattered in a randomness determined by each one's position on the slope. However, the buildings remain tightly connected through corridors that snake upwards to the library along breezy walkways and landscaped courts. A four-storey student hostel is set apart from this central complex across an informal amphi-theatre fashioned from excess building material, and made by merely consolidating the contours. Further down is a students' canteen and a girls' hostel. At the far end, near the entrance

161

gate, are located varying densities of staff housing.

Building textures, configurations and spanning elements demonstrate Baker's easy manipulation of brick, all of which were made close to the site and fired with locally-available coconut palm wood. All

surfaces, whether inside or out, in the dormitory or classroom, are exposed to patterns showing varying bonding techniques and *jali* work. Openings are arched, corbelled or spanned with brick lintels. The same attitude of experimentation is seen in walls that are stepped, curved or folded for added strength; wall thicknesses change on different floors, depending on the loading and requirement.

In Baker's buildings, heights are kept deliberately low and much below the tree-line. The height of the coconut palm had once provided an unwritten restriction for traditional buildings in Kerala, and Baker has rigorously conformed to this limit. Even in his institutional complexes, the land is rarely exploited to create man-made geometries or monumental axes and relationships. At the Centre all buildings are located along the slope of the hill, taking their shapes from the disposition of the land. Connections between them are along brick-walkways lined with lights having brick supports.

Men's Hostel
Centre for Development Studies

That the architecture can demonstrate, in a direct and practical way, the economic goals of an institute, is seen in the simplified design of the specific buildings on the campus of the Centre for Development Studies. In the men's hostel this economy is expressed in the organization of the plan, the nature of the construction and the materials used.

Eight rooms in a single file opening onto a veranda, and four stacked floors give a formidable linear shape to the plan. Each room is entered simply down a rear corridor built into the shared walls. This inordinately regimented organization is offset by the playfulness of the circulation and the entrance block—both of which move away from an excessive rectilinearity into the magical realm of curved walls, circular staircases and deep-set wall-niches. Though the composition at a close range

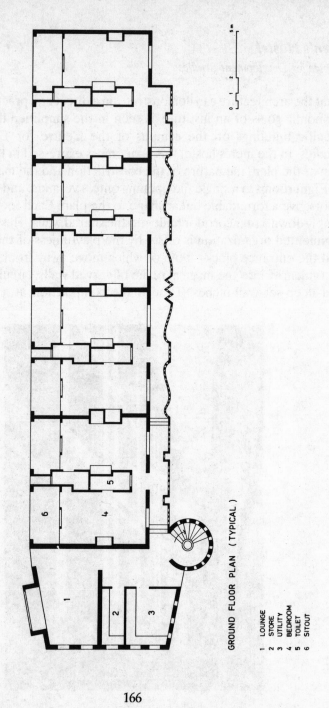

GROUND FLOOR PLAN (TYPICAL)

1 LOUNGE
2 STORE
3 UTILITY
4 BEDROOM
5 TOILET
6 SITOUT

interior

makes for startling contrasts of light and shade, Baker's justification remains purely structural and economic, 'I was very keen to demonstrate the use of four-and-a-half inch thick load-bearing wall. When such a wall is taken to four storeys the curves and circles give it that added stiffness.'

Local problems of environmental degradation led Baker to experiment with materials as well. He says, 'In those days bricks were plentiful, well burnt and reasonably inexpensive. Unfortunately in Kerala, bricks are fired with wood, which led to forest destruction, so I gave preference to fuel-free materials, like stone laterite and mud.'

Random rubble mixed in lime *surkhi* mortar (lime manufactured from sea shells on the site) was used in the construction of the foundation; and load-bearing brick was used in the super structure. All slabs are of filler tiles, the flooring a mixture of local quarry tiles, and the windows of jackwood. Plastering is found only in the bathrooms—all the other surfaces being either exposed or whitewashed. The circular stair tower incorporates pre-cast stair treads using filler slab and bamboo reinforcement.

Women's Hostel
Centre for Development Studies

Explaining how this building came up, Baker says, 'When we started building the Centre there were not many women on the faculty who needed accommodation. So the first women's hostel plan was a small cylindrical building, three storeys high. But an enlightened establishment like the Centre soon had a lot of women and the original plan was not enough to house them all. So we built another adjoining hostel on a rather restricted site.'

The rooms, like those of the men's hostel, have the rigid layout of undifferentiated rectangles, opening into the privacy of a forest behind the building. But where Baker had provided the residual spaces of hostel

the circular house

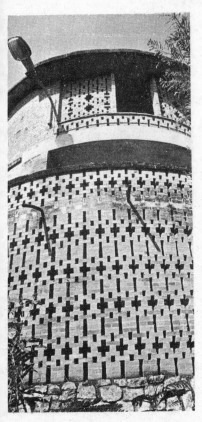

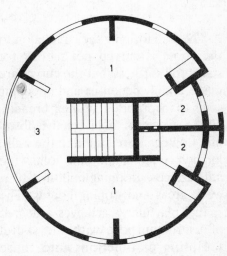

TYPICAL FLOOR PLAN

1 ROOM
2 TOILET
3 BALCONY

0 1 2   5m

169

living as an end block in the men's building, the design here takes on an entirely new spatial dimension. Says Baker, 'This time the room, the balcony and the staircase plan were much more orthodox—but we made the usual connecting corridors very unorthodox by enclosing them in *jali* walls of rather florid building shapes.'

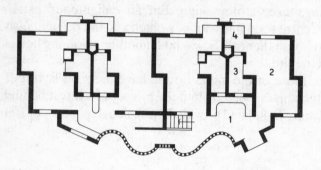

GROUND FLOOR PLAN (TYPICAL)

1 FOYER
2 ROOM
3 TOILET
4 BALCONY

0 1 2   5m

The wall forming the circulation to the room is curved not merely for structural stiffness, but the curves are made unduly generous and sweeping so as to incorporate, in their breadth, all the spaces for an interactive hostel life. Low seats are built into the walls; kitchen counters and sinks follow the *jali* surfaces, dropping built-in tables, work areas and ironing boards. The spatial playfulness achieves a degree of useful purpose with the skilful sculpting of functions into these spaces.

undulating house

170

Computer Centre
Centre for Development Studies

Later, Baker was approached to design the new premises to accommodate a computer at the Centre. How does a setting, designed on the principle of open lattice wall planning, breezeways and built of natural brick and stone, allow for the introduction of electronic sophistication, and the strict environmental controls required for a computer facility?

exterior wall details

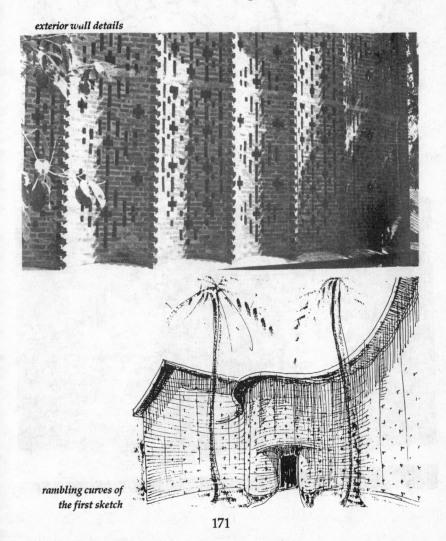

*rambling curves of
the first sketch*

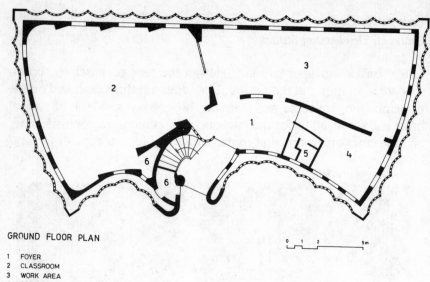

GROUND FLOOR PLAN

1 FOYER
2 CLASSROOM
3 WORK AREA
4 OFFICE
5 TOILET
6 STORE

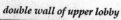

double wall of upper lobby

172

For Baker this was a double-edged problem, for the solution not only called for a simple resolution of the requirements but also an appropriate one fitting in naturally and harmoniously with the elevations of the twenty-five-year-old institution.

Baker's answer was a double-walled building with an outer surface of intersecting circles of brick *jalis* which followed the design of the main academic block, while the internal shell fulfilled the constraints and controls necessary for a computer laboratory. The space between the two walls accommodated the secondary requirements for offices and storage areas.

The two storey-high outer wall of single-brick thickness is stiffened by a series of intersecting circle segments; the mid-level slab is also fused into it for additional support. The pattern of perforations, unrelieved across the four faces of the building are like computer punch-outs and so suggestive of the functions they house. Larger corbelled window-openings of the inner wall control the diffused light of the outer wall and create a continuous glare-free atmosphere. A low entrance of the perforated wall cuts into the centre and directs the visitor up into a lobby lit by a skylight. The roof is a folded concrete slab.

173

Loyola Chapel and Auditorium
Sreekarayam, 1971

On a small college campus, on the outskirts of Trivandrum, is another group of Baker's buildings, built on the scale of the Centre for Development Studies. Though the site was not planned and developed entirely by Baker, he designed individual projects such as dormitories, classrooms, field-house and larger ceremonial structures of a collective nature.

The Loyala complex contains a high school and a post-graduate complex, both sharing a common chapel and an auditorium. It was here

windowless cavity wall:
the wall is double with a
cavity between the two skins

	Rate		Quantity	Figure	Say
Excavation and refilling	cu.ft.	0.06	16,000	960	1,000
Concrete foundations 1:4:8	cu.ft.	1.20	1,900	2,280	2,500
DPC:CM 1:3 crude oil 5% wt c.	sq.ft.	0.30	560	168	200
RR masonry in 1:5 cm	cu.ft.	0.95	3,360	3,192	3,300
first class bricks in 1:5 cm	cu.ft.	1.80	16,100	28,980	29,000
4.5" brick in 1:4 cm	sq.ft.	0.75	1,250	938	1,000
ditto query extra	sq.ft.	0.75	1,600	1,200	1,500
flooring 4"1:4:8 plus c.finish	sq.ft.	0.65	6,840	4,480	4,500
slab floor c. finish					500
0.5" cm plaster	sq.ft.	0.22	11,860	2,609	3,000
3 coat whitewashing	sq.ft.	0.03	11,860	355	500
Supercem 3 coats (2 and primer)	sq.ft.	0.30	11,860	3,560	4,000
RC frame	cu.ft.	11.00		8,500	8,500
RC slabs	cu.ft.	8.00	2,560	20,480	20,500
Doors					5,000
Windows					500
Chapel ceiling					10,000
Auditorium ceiling					7,500
Roof weathering 3" jelly tiles etc.	sq.ft.	1.50	1,150	1,725	2,000
AC roofing	sq.ft.	1.50	6,050	9,075	9,000
Steel trusses	cu.wt.	115.			25,000
Sanitation and drains					2,500
Electrical installation					10,000
3% contingencies				4,425	4,500
Furniture for chapel					18,000
Total					Rs 1,70,000

L.W. Baker, A.R.I.B.A., October 1969

that Baker's skills of cost-reduction met their greatest challenge, as it required a seating capacity of one thousand. In an attempt to construct both the auditorium and the chapel within the budget for only one building Baker realized that the cost of placing one large hall above the other would be far too expensive. 'I proposed instead to put them side by side, and decided that the biggest cost-reducing factor would be to avoid the use of steel and reinforced concrete, and to use load-bearing walls with a timber roof frame carrying an asbestos sheet roof.'

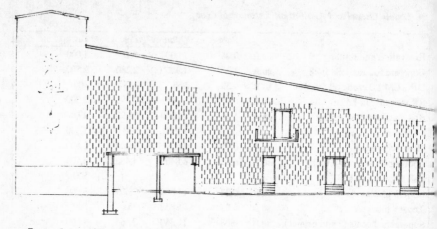

In order to increase the lateral strength of the high brick wall, without the introduction of any steel or concrete, Baker devised a wide cavity double-wall with cross-bracing brick. Both the walls were pierced with a continuous floor-to-roof pattern of *jalis*, so that the chapel was adequately, though somewhat mysteriously, lit and ventilated. Despite its tall proportions, the acoustics of the hall were remarkable—the exposed surfaces and the open patterns of brickwork controlling the

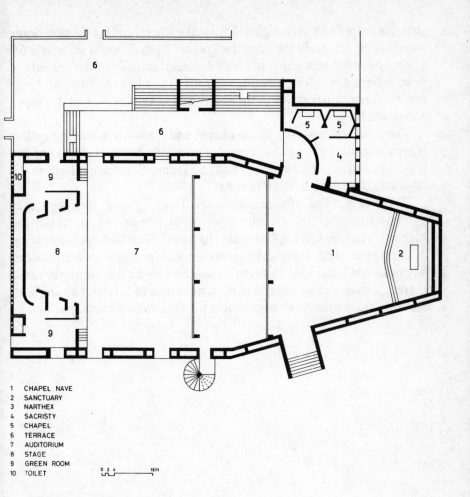

1	CHAPEL NAVE
2	SANCTUARY
3	NARTHEX
4	SACRISTY
5	CHAPEL
6	TERRACE
7	AUDITORIUM
8	STAGE
9	GREEN ROOM
10	TOILET

reverberations.

One of things Baker deplores about contemporary brick building practices is the cubist approach that avoids any sort of capping or overhangs to wall tops which leads to the walls getting badly stained and streaked in a very short time. So he insisted on a protruding top chord of the wooden trusses. This carries a two-foot overhang of the asbestos sheeting roof and protects the ends of the wooden members by adding a strip of fascia.

One of the conditions specified was that the chapel must not dwarf the existing three-storeyed buildings surrounding it. And yet, the fact that the chapel had to be high did not make it essential for the remaining structure to maintain the same height. So from a height of nearly 6.5 metres over the sanctuary, the roof descends steadily to the rear of the nave, where it is still high enough to roof the gallery of the auditorium; and then continues down to the stage, and at the far rear to the green room and lavatories.

The total covered area of the chapel and auditorium and the gallery is approximately 930 square metres. The cost in 1970–71, including the furniture and appurtenances, lighting and sanitation was kept within the original gift sum of 1.75 lakh rupees.

Baker says, 'The official clients are Jesuit priests. Although they agreed to my proposals and plans, obviously they did not appreciate the high vast stretches of unplastered brickwork. They had every intention of tarting the whole thing up later on with nice bright paints and plasters, but have not been able to bring themselves to do this simply because there is a small but steady and persistent stream of foreign visitors, both architects and priests, who come just to see and take photographs.'

Loyola Graduate Women's Hostel
Sreekarayam, Trivandrum, 1970

This was Baker's first institutional project in Trivandrum, and it incorporates in it all the characteristics of his architecture. Open brick walls, corbelled brackets and traditional fish-tile roofs combine in a series of linked arcaded courts set along a slope.

An important requirement had been a quiet seclusion within which the women could follow a strict Christian regimen. 'They were to be guarded from any outside intrusion by devoted and determined nuns,' says Baker. 'Gates were to close at sunset; no windows to overlook the street. Study games, recreation, meditation and exercises were all to be done within high protective walls.'

For Baker it was necessary that the 'prison-like feeling' that accompanies such introversion, be counteracted by the creation of an 'outdoors' within the indoors. So, the sense of being held captive needed to be dispersed in a series of places built within the confining outer walls.

terracotta roofscape

entran

This was dealt with using a 'checker-board plan, in which the black squares became the hostel buildings and the white ones, the gardens, pools, courts and sit-arounds under trees'. Baker sought to provide the intimate scale of a shared house within the conventional hostel plan.

Baker says, 'The girls didn't want single rooms, and I had already discovered while doing other hostels, that they preferred the safety and comfort of a cottage. So I devised a plan with six nooks within a large shared room—each nook big enough for a bed, a desk, a cupboard, a seat or two but with only three walls to each nook and the south wall open into a common central area.

'The final hurdle to get over was that when we presented the checker

an 'outdoors' within the indoors

181

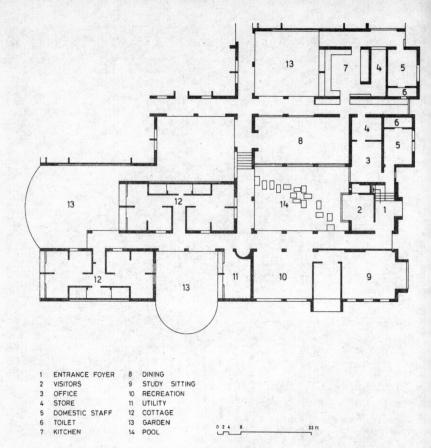

1	ENTRANCE FOYER	8	DINING
2	VISITORS	9	STUDY SITTING
3	OFFICE	10	RECREATION
4	STORE	11	UTILITY
5	DOMESTIC STAFF	12	COTTAGE
6	TOILET	13	GARDEN
7	KITCHEN	14	POOL

board plan to the University Grants Commission(UGC) they said "whatever is this? You said you wanted a Hostel! This looks like holiday cottages on the beach. A hostel is a row of rooms along a corridor with the usual services and stairs at one end or the other..."

'It took a long time to persuade them that this was not only a more suitable hostel but a much cheaper one. "Nonsense"—they retorted again—"the University Engineer had better do your estimates for you." His estimates were double mine and yet we had fulfilled the UGC requirements. And so, we built the hostel for our original estimate—and never had the final phase payment because we had added so many odd desirable extra rooms that were not down on the UGC list of what a Graduate Women's Hostel should have.'

182

St. John's Cathedral
Tiruvella, 1973–74

Christianity came to Kerala nearly 200 years ago. It is not known what sort of architecture was used in the early church buildings, but most likely local wood, bamboo, thatch, and soft laterite stone were used for their building. Presumably an impermanent local style of architecture developed out of these materials and it probably resembled the traditional bamboo constructions used by the Hindus in their religious buildings. But in Kerala's hot and humid, tropical climate, timber and bamboo deteriorate quickly and buildings would have been constantly in a state of repair or renewal. Many centuries later, the Portuguese, the Dutch and other European colonizers brought with them—what they believed to be—a proper Church architecture. The fact that this imported style is the only religious Christian architecture that remains in Kerala today almost certainly means that they disapproved of whatever indigenous church architecture they found here.

However, after attending the Second Vatican Council in Rome, the

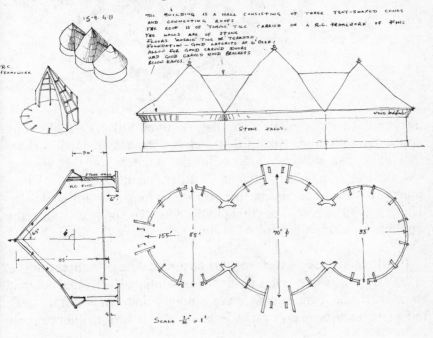

183

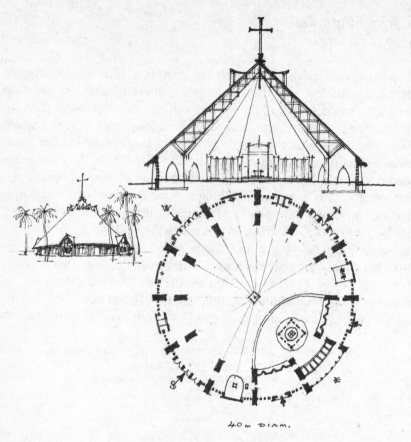

40m DIAM.

Bishop of Tiruvella, Mar Athenasios, returned to Kerala inspired by Pope John's pronouncements that each country should build its churches in its own indigenous style. But the problem was that nothing remained of Kerala's indigenous Christian architectural style. Every church, however old, was in the western Baroque or Gothic design. There was not a hint of anything indigenous. The people themselves would point to the western-styled churches and say 'this is our Kerala style'.

Laurie Baker sought the probable historical developments after the apostle Thomas came to Kerala in the first century. He pointed out that the local Hindu temple architecture is not a 'Hindu' or a 'Kerala' one, but a functional bamboo style and has its counterparts in other tropical

184

bamboo-growing countries. He demonstrated, with sketches, how the bamboo architectural style could be modified for the Christian requirements. After a great deal of research and experimental sketches, the Bishop agreed that the effort could be adapted to the construction of St. John's

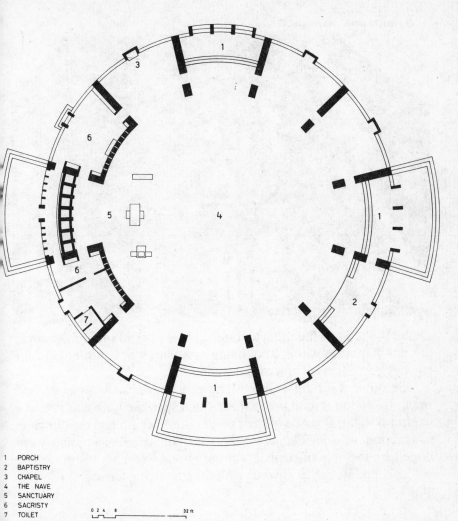

1	PORCH
2	BAPTISTRY
3	CHAPEL
4	THE NAVE
5	SANCTUARY
6	SACRISTY
7	TOILET

0 2 4 8   32 ft

Cathedral.

Interestingly enough, the people accepted this idea more readily than most of the clergy who resisted it, mainly because of the building's close resemblance to some of the big local Hindu temples. But Baker's cathedral only reinforces the idea of recreating the centrally-planned church in a vernacular idiom. In a circular plan of approximately 120-feet diameter, the building combines the internal organization of a Greek-cross with the external appearance of a Hindu temple. However,

187

unlike the temple, the drum and the steeply pitched roof of the circle are not contained within a confining ambulatory or court, but are set squarely in the centre of a walled compound.

The outer walls are built entirely of locally-available granite and brick. Jackwood is used in the trusses that span the walls and rise to a central skylight. Because of their seventy-foot length and the difficulty of erection, working details for the truss laminations and joints were done with the help of engineers at the Forest Research Institute. The roof, pitched steeply, is covered with the traditional terracotta fish-tile.

Nalanda State Institute of Languages
Nandankode, Trivandrum, 1973

Laurie Baker was asked to produce a design for this institute, which temporarily functioned out of a tiny house consisting of the main room and verandas accommodating the printing machinery. The translators were housed in bathrooms. Baker says, 'The Director had approached me in desperation asking if I could do a simple building within a month for his printing presses while they could continue to use the house as the office.'

Baker's project, when completed, demonstrated both the practicality of construction within the prescribed budget, as well as the ability of meeting the one-month deadline. This was achieved in the reductive simplicity of the buildings which form the complex. The architecture has a barn-like austerity; the repetitive profiles of the roof, the rhythm of the windows and the continual texture of unrelieved walls suggest an industrial assembly-line. Exposed brick is used throughout in staggered bonds of half-brick thick walls. The recesses and rough textures, the architect felt, made little difference in a place accommodating

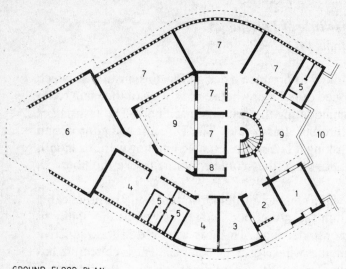

GROUND FLOOR PLAN

FIRST FLOOR P

1	BOOK SHOP	6	HALL
2	FOYER	7	ROOM
3	OFFICE	8	STORE
4	STAFF	9	OPEN GARDEN
5	TOILET	10	EXISTING BUILDING

Nalanda State Institute of Languages: Estimate of Cost

	Quantity and Rate	Appx. Cost
Basement	2.900 cu.ft. RR @ (130) 90	2,610
Exc.	1.400 @ 80(90)	112
Brickwork	5.000 cu.ft. @ 160(200)	9,000
Flooring	4.100 sq.ft. @ 80 (90)	3,280
Special roof	1.600 sq.ft. @ 2	3,200
Mang. tile roof	5.500 sq.ft. @ 140 (160)	7,700
Plaster	2.000 sq.ft. @ 20	400
Doors and windows		12,600
Total	Rs	38,902

mechanized production. The high walls, toned with a colour wash, support combinations of wooden truss and tile roofs as well as Baker's filler slab. Their spatial organization too, very simply reflects the printing process in a single file plan and is set on the relatively flat site surrounding the old house.

190

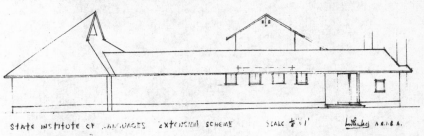

STATE INSTITUTE OF LANGUAGES EXTENSION SCHEME   SCALE ⅛"=1'   Len Bailey A.R.I.B.A.

Chitralekha Film Studio
Aakulam, Trivandrum, 1974–76

A film studio is an unlikely commission for an architect who has devoted a lifetime to low-cost shelter. But the building was built at the request of Adoor Gopalakrishnan, a friend, and one of the country's more sensitive film-makers.

The complex is sited on a promontory on one of Baker's more dramatic locations. Overlooking vast stretches of paddy fields, the distant ocean and a neighbouring hill, the building is dispersed into fragments that take advantage of this spectacular view. Unlike a conventional studio where the focus is strictly contained within a building envelope so as to control the fiction of filming, Baker split the complex into its residual parts: filming, editing, scripting, library, administration—and then made the necessary connections across verandas and courts.

For the visitor, there is an air of the stage set even in the buildings. The approach from the road is along a high wall with the usual Baker bonding, which terminates at the gate into a traditional turret and a watchman's cabin. From here, the road curves gently uphill and reveals the two predominant architectural features of the complex: a wide

192

two-storey tower with a conference room above and a low entrance portico, a wooden remnant from a temple which has been incorporated into the front wall.

temple portico as studio entrance

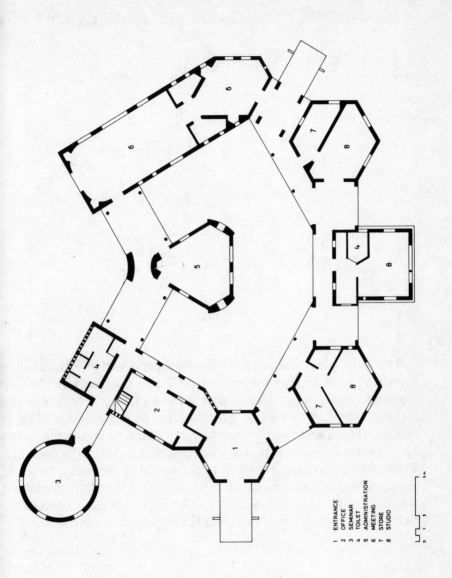

1 ENTRANCE
2 OFFICE
3 SEMINAR
4 TOILET
5 ADMINISTRATION
6 MEETING
7 STORE
8 STUDIO

195

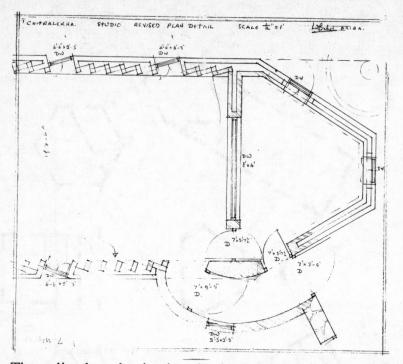

The split plan, dominating the landscape with its controlling
geometry, is yet another departure from Baker's normal style. Where
the site topography provides no clue to the anchoring of buildings, the
architect has had to turn to geometry for its organization. This is
assiduously accomplished by the numerous hexagons connected by the
arched veranda, and oriented towards different slopes of the same hill.
The buildings are built entirely of brick bonded in alternating bands of
plastered and exposed brickwork. The roofs, sloped and self-contained
over each room, are of fish-tiles. An intriguing composition of concrete
medallions is incorporated in the wall of the entrance court.

Corpus Christi School
Kottayam, 1972

If a house can suggest the idiosyncracies of its resident then an institutional project should also reflect the attributes of the institution in its architecture. At the Centre for Development Studies (p.160) Baker's expression was consistent with the cost-effective economics and policies of development. Here, at the Corpus Cristi School, the nature of a child's experience in learning and play is reflected in a plan that itself suggests a playful inquiry.

The straight line and excessive rectilinearity may not directly offend a child's sensibility but Baker feels the meandering wall, the circle and square as counterpoint, make for a more desirable and inhabitable landscape. Where rooms do not have the formal labels of classroom, assembly hall or office, the student feels less intimidated and is left free to roam, to meet others like himself, and discover places suitable for learning and play.

The site along a gentle hill is graded into a series of related plateaus. The upper contours, serviceable from the road, contain the formal

entrance and the administrative block

197

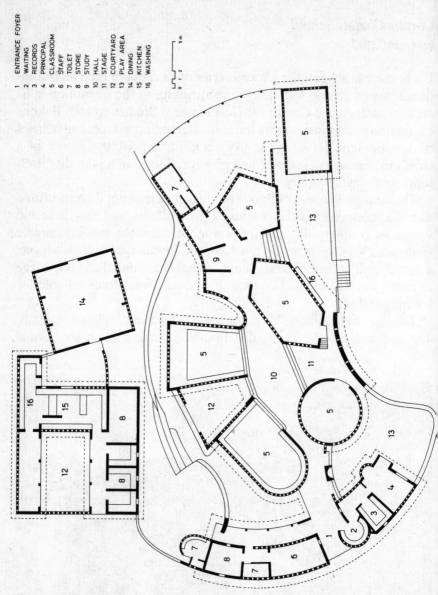

KEY

1 ENTRANCE FOYER
2 WAITING
3 RECORDS
4 PRINCIPAL
5 CLASSROOM
6 STAFF
7 TOILET
8 STORE
9 STUDY
10 HALL
11 STAGE
12 COURTYARD
13 PLAY AREA
14 DINING
15 KITCHEN
16 WASHING

0 1 2 5 m

functions of kitchen and services in a rectangular courtyard building, the dining hall breaking free from the composition. On lower ground, the rooms twist, turn and triangulate into varying positions and sizes,

offering choices of formal classrooms as well as intimate study dens, larger halls and smaller nooks. The playfulness of the walls, however, reveal a delicately worked flexibility. Rooms function as independent classrooms, but, when necessary, their radiating walls also serve to shift the focus to the gallery outside, and, together, the teaching complex becomes a single multipurpose hall.

The success of the project is doubtlessly the outcome of an architecture that itself encourages innovative teaching; this is also apparent in the rapid expansion programme and the increasing enrolment of students in the school.

Children's Village

near Nagercoil, Tamilnadu, 1965

This small institution for orphans was set up at the personal request of a philanthropic German. The institution now forms part of a countrywide chain of similar institutions supported by the Christian Mission Service.

Ten to twelve boys and girls between the ages of three and sixteen live in a single house. Each house is designed as a self-contained unit, comprising of a room for the house mother, dormitories for the children and a bathroom and kitchen block—all organized around fronting verandas and a courtyard. The several similar houses on the site vary subtly to accommodate the topography. Though numerous additions and sub-divisions have been made since the original construction, the buildings still retain the character of a courtyard dormitory, in which the children live as a large family.

The complex has all the components of an institution, and yet the architecture has none of the forbidding heirarchy and enclosure of one. Baker has deliberately chosen a building image compatible with a large house, low and dispersed on the gently sloping contours, to provide a docile setting for the children traumatized by parental loss. For the children, the 'tucking in' of the buildings—classrooms, dining hall, bath houses—into the forest makes for an organization where nature

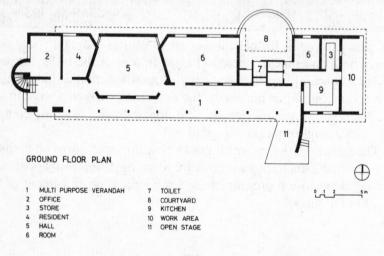

GROUND FLOOR PLAN

1	MULTI PURPOSE VERANDAH	7 TOILET
2	OFFICE	8 COURTYARD
3	STORE	9 KITCHEN
4	RESIDENT	10 WORK AREA
5	HALL	11 OPEN STAGE
6	ROOM	

200

dominates the built form. This may be disconcerting to a visitor who could lose his way in the complex, but the permanent residents of staff and the children find the green landscape a congenial backdrop to the buildings.

In virtually all of Baker's institutional work, the architecture has an uncertain, almost unfelt, presence, backed by a conviction that buildings—whatever their function—are secondary to the surroundings and sustained only by their natural harmony with environment. This is so even in those institutions where convention ordinarily dictates that the organization be clear and discernable.

Fishermen's Village
Poonthura, Trivandrum, 1974–75

In tribal societies, where the erection of shelter is a labour shared by the community, where the making and reshaping of homes is a consequence

an alternative design

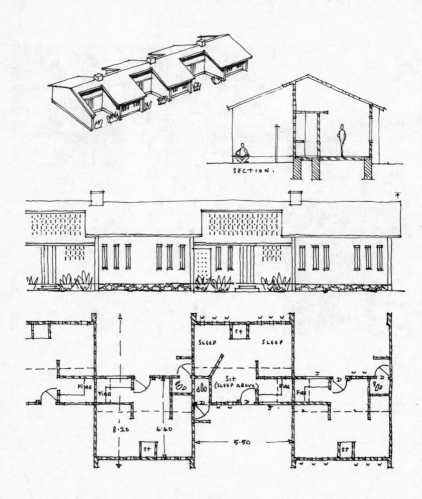

250 SQ FT (25·0 m²) ROW HOUSES   SCALE 1:100

SECTION.

SLEEP   Sit   SLEEP

FIRE   FIRE   Sit (SLEEP ABOVE)   FIRE   FIRE

8·20   4·40   5·50

of the strong ties of kinship, the insular family and caste organization—the mediation of an outside architect can hardly be welcome. Moreover, the severity of the environment in which the tribals live and the limitation of their resources, impose restrictions that have kept most of the 'conventional architects away from such projects.

Paradoxically, these were the reasons that brought Baker into the project for displaced fishermen in Trivandrum. Baker says, 'It was an unusual project. Every year some village or the other in Kerala gets washed away and every year they get an enormous amount as compensation money for clothing and blankets and may be even some for the replacement of huts.'

Baker felt that the amount spent every year on rehabilitation could be more usefully directed into the construction of permanent houses, designed and oriented to counter the effect of cyclones. With the support of the Chief Minister he proceeded to survey, design and build on land newly acquired near the old site. It was during this time that Baker realized the difficulties of dealing with large insular groups, with set ideas and tradition. He recalls, 'I didn't have much time to study the project. They were all so distressed over the storm damage and we had

to get the houses up as quickly as possible; and we mainly wanted to demonstrate that such permanent structures could be put up quickly.'

Though the materials, the exposed brickwork and structure, and the sloped concrete roofs, are similar to Baker's other projects, the unique innovation here is the openness of design and the way individual units offset each other. The cyclonic wind meets no resistance and is allowed to pass through the house by the continuous lattice work in the exposed walls. The low sloped roofs and courts serve as wind-catchers, and the open walls function to dispel it. The long row of conventional housing is replaced by an even staggering, so that fronting courts catch the breeze and also get a view of the sea, and at the same time 'there are little private rectangles of land in between the houses where they can dry the nets and kids can play'. Since a good part of a fisherman's life is spent out of doors, the house and court function admirably—providing sleeping lofts within, and adequate space outside for mending nets and cleaning and drying fish.

Though the project was built and occupied as planned, there remained in it, a certain sense of incompleteness. Besides the houses, there was little else on the site—community structures, shared facilities, or even a confining boundary—that could suggest a heirarchy. But this is perhaps a shortcoming in most experimental work, and the inability of a professional to comprehend the underlying patterns of a tribal group and to respond to its private needs.

Tourist Centre

Ponmudi, 1980

The former Chief Minister of Kerala, Achuta Menon, proposed the setting up of a health resort for Trivandrum on the 3000-foot high peak at Ponmudi, sixty kilometers from the city. Baker was asked to submit a scheme for the complex to be built by the Public Works Department (PWD) and supervised—to pacify the auditors—by a government chief engineer.

On the dramatic slope, strewn with boulders and devoid of all vegetation, Baker planned a series of isolated cottages stepping up the

the concrete-pyramid-capped cottage

gradient. 'I thought of them as rocks dropping and anchoring to a cliff,' says Baker.

Baker's view of the tourist scheme

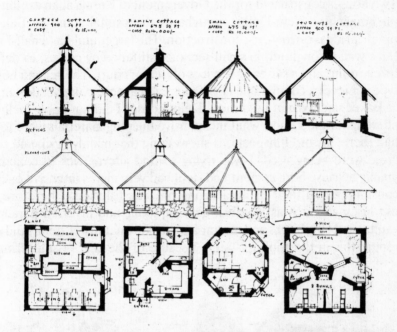

With a uniform stone elevation capped by a concrete pyramid, the architecture of the cottage reinforces the image of rugged materials assembled in clear simple forms. But inside, each rock assumes the home-like comfort of a snug retreat. An exterior face of rough random rubble gives way to designs of varying shapes and dimensions: a square plan accommodates bunks for students, an octagon for a couple, and a smaller square for a family.

Experimental Houses
New Delhi, 1980

Two houses constructed for the Government of Kerala at an exhibition on housing at New Delhi, brought to the capital some of Baker's practical ideas on low-cost construction. The larger unit has a half-brick thick wall throughout, in small sections, stiffened by curves, to define three rooms and a series of services off a rear court. The second house type achieves a comparable covered area in a more compact design.

Baker said, 'When I did these Delhi houses I did not know Delhi at all well, nor did I know what inexpensive building materials were to be had there; my brief inspections showed me that mainly brick and concrete were being used. I was trying to find alternatives to concrete, mainly because both cement and steel had very highly intensive energy consumption in their manufacturing process. I decided, therefore, to use brick as much as possible. The parabolic and inverted parabolic vaults used only bricks and mortar and a small quantity of steel. I did not repeat this in the roofing system because of the cost of shuttering—

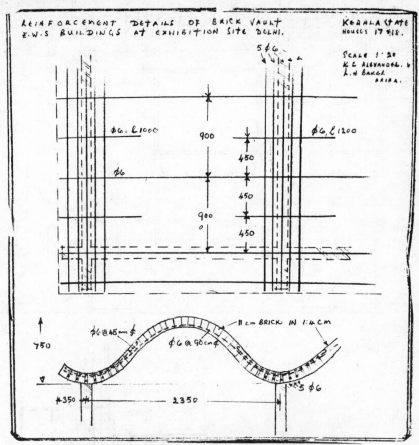

REINFORCEMENT DETAILS OF BRICK VAULT
E.W.S BUILDINGS AT EXHIBITION SITE DELHI.

KERALA STATE
HOUSES 17 & 18.

SCALE 1:20
K.C. ALEXANDER &
L.W BAKER
ARIBA.

5 φ6

φ6. ℓ1000   900   φ6, ℓ1200

φ6   450

450

900   450
0

750

φ6 @ 45 cm φ   11 cm BRICK IN 1:4 CM

φ6 @ 90 cm φ

350   2350   5 φ6

209

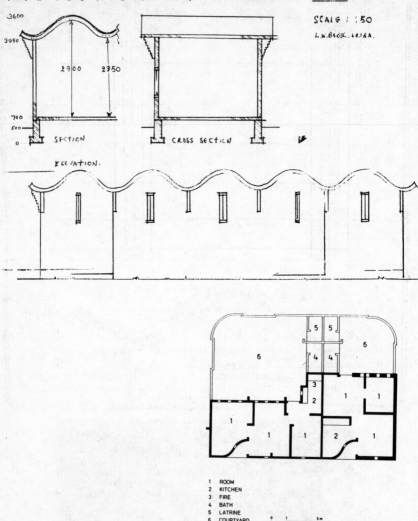

TWO DEMONSTRATION LOW COST HOUSES FOR THE KERALA GOVERNMENT AT THE N.E.O & D.D.A. EXHIBITION AT NEW DELHI. REVISED PLAN!

SCALE 1 : 50

L.W.BAKER. 16.16A.

SECTION

CROSS SECTION

ELEVATION.

1 ROOM
2 KITCHEN
3 FIRE
4 BATH
5 LATRINE
6 COURTYARD

though I am sure for a colony or a large number of standard-sized buildings re-usable form-work could be devised and used.'

210

Anganwadis
Trivandrum District, 1984

As part of the district program to promote informal education, the state

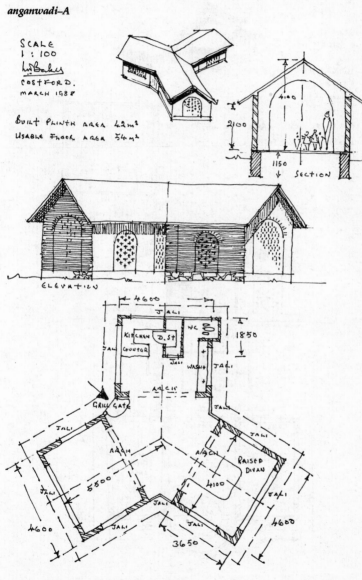

anganwadi–A

SCALE
1 : 100
L. Baker
COSTFORD.
MARCH 1988

Built PLINTH AREA 42 m²
USABLE FLOOR AREA 54 m²

SECTION

ELEVATION

government proposed the construction of a number of low-cost day-care centres. The implementation of the program was entrusted to the Centre of Science and Technology for Rural Developing

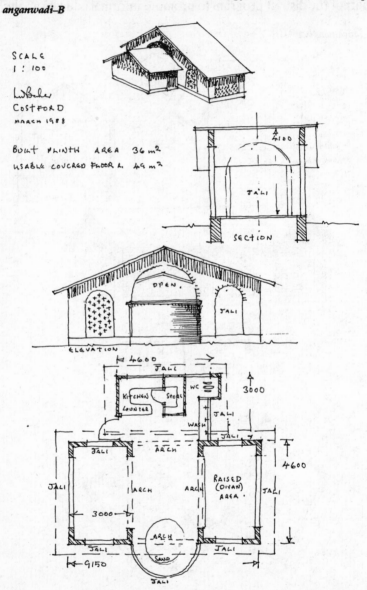

anganwadi-B

SCALE
1 : 100

L.D.Baker
COSTFORD
MARCH 1988

BUILT PLINTH AREA 36 m²
USABLE COVERED FLOOR A. 49 m²

SECTION

ELEVATION

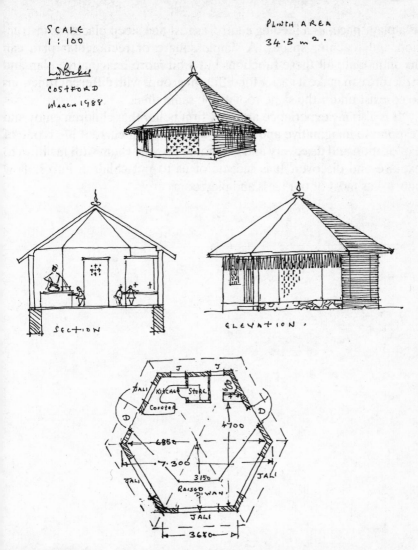

SCALE
1 : 100

PLINTH AREA
34.5 m².

COSTFORD
March 1988

SECTION

ELEVATION

JALI KITCHEN STORE
Counter
JALI
D
4700
6850
7.300
3150
JALI
JALI
RAISED DIWAN
JALI
3680

(COSTFORD), a non-profit organization that helped propogate Baker's ideas. The initial sketches for the buildings demonstrated a number of alternatives that could be adapted to different locations and site conditions.

Expressing his ideas on the designing of these centres, Baker said, 'I feel sure these small buildings, to be built with a very limited amount of money, must be as multipurpose as possible. They are used as shelter, as a play-space, as a feeding centre, as rest and sleep places, as instruction and teaching-spaces. A simple square or rectangular plan can accommodate all these functions but a bit more imaginative plan and structure can make it easier for different groups with different functions to co-exist under the same roof at the same time.

'It is also my experience and very firm belief that children enjoy and respond to imaginative and exciting spaces. Their current life is one of exploration and discovery and we should provide them with facilities to explore and discover. It is sadistic of us to put children into hollow cubes—as most of our class and playrooms are!'

Nirmithi Kendra
Aakulam, Trivandrum, 1987

The task of disseminating low-cost building technology appropriate to

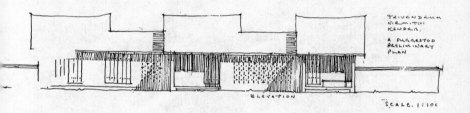

suggested plan

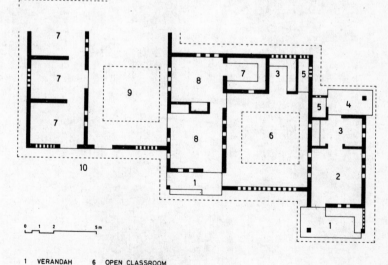

1	VERANDAH	6	OPEN CLASSROOM
2	LIVING	7	STORE
3	KITCHEN	8	OFFICE
4	WORK AREA	9	PARTLY OPEN WORK YARD
5	TOILET	10	UNLOADING PLATFORM

each district was taken up by the state government through the establishment of training and demonstration centres called Nirmithi Kendras. Sketches for the first Kendra, built in Trivandrum, were prepared by Baker and later developed by architects of the Building Centre.

Office and teaching accommodation were provided for in a building that itself set an example of the ideas it was meant to illustrate: alternatives, local inexpensive materials and construction techniques.

Baker feels, 'Nothing must be done at the Kendra and in the buildings of the Kendra that ordinary people cannot acquire and do for themselves. The buildings must demonstrate the construction possibilities of a really low-cost building which is acceptable and beautiful, which is functional and suitable for the Trivandrum district, and which uses minimum energy (fuel) in manufacture of materials for building techniques and for maintenance. It must clearly demonstrate that 'low-cost' does not reduce or lessen structural stability and durability and that it is more maintenance-free than the conventional fashionable buildings. The current costs of all materials used and all labour employed in production must be clearly shown so that all can understand how cost-reduction is achieved.'

217

Section III

WRITINGS

Writings

A commonly held belief among architects is that a work of architecture never lives up to the ideas that have generated it. This is a belief held by architects whose thoughts and design conceptions expressed on paper suffer, for whatever reasons, unfortunate transformations on the building site. However, Baker's architecture on paper expresses exactly what he actually builds. Sketches, drawings and the notes alongside carry the conviction of a pen on to the site. Moreover, the strength of an architect's work lies as much in his buildings as in the thoughts that have generated them. As an architect, Baker's first commitment is to building, but, as he willingly admits, his architecture is the result of a personal ideology of honesty, a spartan simplicity that expresses itself in his work and life, in his ways of building, of dealing with people, of living and reacting with the members of his own family. A deep-rooted commitment to place and context is perhaps the outcome of a professional practice centred over extended periods in a single area—first the seventeen years in Pithoragarh in the Garhwal hills and the last twenty-six-odd years in Trivandrum in south Kerala.

Besides similarities of design approaches in both these places, evidence of Baker's vision is seen in his numerous published and unpublished articles, papers and seminar reports. They reflect his attitude towards conservation, of both materials and heritage; they suggest methods of architectural documentation; and they establish simplified methods for national housing programmes, in their administration and technology. In abstraction, a combination of all these ideas provides clues to what could be a common approach to building in India, and in other developing countries. The articles also express Baker's continuing quest for an architecture relevant to our times.

What an architect builds and how he does so is to a great extent influenced by what he sees, experiences and records. Baker's eye for detail, the personal unique finish, fulfilling individual needs in the homes that he creates for his clients, are also evident in the sensitivity of his record of vernacular architecture.

This, the third section of the book begins with the architect's perception of his own architecture and an appreciation of vernacular architecture as recorded in his personal experience in Pithoragarh and Kerala. A comprehension of the changing condition in the economics of building is expressed in Baker's articles on the adaptation of new technologies to the vernacular, and vice versa, the application of vernacular principles to new methods of construction. In 'Does Cost-Reduction Mean Poor Quality?' and 'Is a Modern Indian Architecture Possible?', Baker suggests the inevitability of change without a sentimental attachment to the past.

Baker on 'Laurie Baker' Architecture

I stayed with Quaker friends who were close to Gandhiji and had the thrill and the blessing of talking with him about the lives of people in India and China. It was strange to spend time demonstrating and explaining to him how my Chinese cloth shoes were made and then later to have 'Quit India' shouted after me as I returned through the streets to the house where I was staying. During this period of enforced stay in India, I saw mansions and I saw slums. I met very great people and I mixed with many very poor, lowly people. I talked with Gandhiji about my urge to return to work in India even though the British were being urged to get out and was encouraged by him to return to India. However, I finally returned to war-torn Birmingham. Obviously there was going to be a major requirement of architects once the war came to an end. Even so, the housing needs of many of the millions of people in India seemed to be far greater and their chances of getting people to help them build extensively far lesser than those in Britain.

So, within a few months, I found myself on board a ship bound for India. I had been enrolled as an architect for a Mission which was international and interdenominational and whose sole purpose was the care of those suffering from leprosy. On my return I was sent to live in, what were then known as, the United Provinces in north India with an elderly missionary couple who were to 'teach me the ropes'. To my horror I found that I was labelled a 'Sahib', a 'White Man', and an 'Imperialist'! I had to live in a large bungalow with lots of servants and I had to 'dress for dinner' and there was a rigid code of what 'was Done' and what 'was Not Done'. Under this code I could ride a horse but not a bicycle. After two weeks I rebelled, bought a bicycle, and rode off to live with an Indian doctor at the leprosy hospital seven miles away.

There were immediate problems for me. My work was exciting. It took me all over rural India. People who contracted the disease of leprosy were called 'lepers', with all the stigma and terror that the word

223

carries with it. They were segregated and herded away to asylums, probably never again to mix with ordinary people. But during the Second World War a range of new 'modern' drugs were produced and some of them were found to be helpful in the treatment of leprosy. At the same time there also came about a new approach for the treatment of the unfortunate victims of the dreaded disease. If a cure was possible, then hospitals were needed where they could go to with hope for treatment. Then eventually, perhaps, they could return to normal life, instead of being ostracized for the rest of their lives.

My job was mainly to convert or replace these old dreaded asylums with proper modern hospitals and to create the necessary rehabilitation and occupation centres. But there was no precedent for this new approach of treatment. Medical experts were few and far between and inevitably had varying and even conflicting ideas about how to go about the whole new set of problems. Who was to guide me in my work? To whom should I turn to for instructions? Who actually were my clients? Were they the Mission who paid my salary? Or were they the doctors and dedicated workers who worked selflessly for the relief of the suffering of those caught up by this most dreaded of diseases? Or were they the patients themselves?

At this crossroads of my career, I had already made my choice by going on the bicycle to live in the hospital. It was the Mission that paid my salary who also decided how much money was to be used for each project. The doctors had a fair idea of what they required for their work. But finally it were the patients themselves who would actually live in my buildings, and in them regain not only their health but their hope and self-respect, and finally gain a new entry into life. What better clients could one hope for?

Soon I was swamped by a new set of problems. The buildings I was sent to inspect, their construction techniques and materials used, were nothing like the buildings I had been taught about and designed at my school of architecture. I was expected to deal with mud walls and huge cracks. I was confronted with materials I had never heard of, such as laterite. People seemed to think that even cow-dung was an important building material! I was expected to know how to deal with termites, and even bed bugs. I was warned that in a short time *the monsoon* would come. The word was spoken with such awe and fear as though a monsoon were a ferocious, wild beast ready to pounce on me without warning. And, true enough, it *was* like a ferocious, wild beast and it *did* pounce on me with a vengeance!

In fact, during those first few months I felt increasingly ignorant and helpless. I felt less knowledgeable than the stupidest village idiot for he seemed to know what a termite and a monsoon and black cotton soil were. I had brought with me my text books, reference books and construction manuals, but a bundle of comic strips would have been as helpful. What should I do? Go back home where I belonged? The cry of 'Quit India' was louder and stronger now than ever before—would it not be better to quit?

But it was already too late to quit. I might be snowed under with all these impossible and ridiculous problems (were they really the concern of a proper qualified Associate of the Royal Institute of British Architects?), but I was increasingly fascinated by the skills of ordinary, poor, village people working with the most unpromising and crude materials with apparently almost no recognizable tools to make useful everyday buildings and articles. I spent most of my time watching these people build beautiful houses for themselves with mud and small rough stones and bamboo and dried grass and the poorest quality of timber I had ever seen. I saw round conical houses, up to six metres in diameter, built with pieces of timber no longer than a metre-and-a-half. They had round hoop purlins made of bundles of woven small twigs bound together with long fibres extracted from cactus, creepers and vines. Furthermore, these houses were built in areas that faced devastating cyclones every year and very often this type of indigenous architecture had a better chance of survival than the more 'proper' type of structure made of bricks, mortar and reinforced concrete slabs. I had, up till then, never heard of 'stabilized earths', but all over the country I saw mud walls which were treated with a wide variety of materials: from rice husks to bamboo strips and palm fibres for preventing cracks, and various liquids from calcium (lime) water to pigs' urine for coping with other problems related to the use of mud.

The incredible and fascinating part about all this new education I was receiving was that these strange systems were effective, and slowly I realized that many of the answers to my problems, which I thought I could never solve, lay before me and all round me wherever I went. I

225

suppose it took many years before I really understood and wholehear-tedly believed that wherever I went I saw, in the local indigenous style of architecture, the results of thousands of years of research on how to use only immediately-available, local materials to make structurally-stable buildings that could cope with the local climatic conditions, with the local geography and topography, with all the hazards of nature (whether mineral, vegetable, insect, bird or animal), with the possible hostility of neighbours, and that could accommodate all the require-ments of local religious, social and cultural patterns of living. This was an astounding, wonderful and incredible achievement which no modern, twentieth century architect, or people I know of, has ever made.

Columbus is reputed to have discovered America, but a large number of people had been already living there without the publicity of his discovery for a very long time. Similarly, when I made my own little personal discoveries, I realized that I had merely chanced to find an extensive set of building systems which were in no way 'discoveries' to more than five hundred million people! I wanted to make use of this new knowledge in my own work. Perhaps it was as well that my employers brushed it all aside as a romantic notion for I realized I was merely a witness to these apparently endless indigenous skills and was in no way capable of implementing them so early after my 'discoveries'.

Rather reluctantly I had to return to my drawing board and design 'proper' buildings. I can't say that the result of my latest education was wasted. I learnt more about the more acceptable local materials, with new (to me) ways of using burnt brick, stone, tiles and timber. I also used new kinds of mortar and plaster and, as much as possible, tried to design my buildings in such a way that they would not be offensive or unaccep-table to my real clients, the users of the buildings, and so that they would fit in with the local styles and not be an offence to the eyes of the people with whom I had chosen to live with. I think this was probably the second biggest step towards what (if there really is such a thing) is described as a 'Laurie Baker Architecture'.

Meanwhile, the British had quit India and Gandhiji had been assas-sinated, and I was settled in independent India. I got most of my

226

encouragement and not a little inspiration from the wonderful doctor, P. J. Chandy, who had taken me into his home when I had cycled away from the sahib's bungalow in Fyzabad. As he had an equally wonderful doctor sister I married her and we settled down in a remote area of the Himalayas on the borders of Tibet and Nepal. And there, in mainly truly local indigenous style, we built our home, hospital and schools, and we lived there for more than a decade-and-a-half. During this time I did actually acquire quite a lot of those skills which had so fascinated me.

Slowly I began to be drawn back into the more sophisticated world because, strangely enough, as I was busy absorbing these local skills, people from the outside world came up into the Himalayas to get my help. Among them was a wonderful elderly American lady, Welthy Honsinger Fisher, who was concerned about spreading the teaching of adult literacy throughout India. She had the vision of a village which she'd planned to call 'Literacy Village' and it was here she would teach people how to educate adult illiterates. She would train writers on how to write for the newly-literate adults. She would teach how to use drama, puppetry, music and art as teaching methods. But she wanted, what she first described, a real 'Indian villagesque set-up'. Although crippled, and in her seventies, she'd made the long and difficult journey to our hospital in the Himalayas and stayed with us until she had her plans for her Literacy Village. Later I went down and helped her to lay out the site and start building. Some of her friends were trying to start psychiatric work in India. They were an international team but were going to work with and for Indians (the second member of the team was a south Indian psychoanalyst). They too came and dragged me away from my house in the Himalayas because, although they needed up-to-date modern hospital equipment and surroundings, they needed buildings and an atmosphere that would be acceptable and 'right' for the mentally-disturbed Indian patients. Naturally, as a pioneer work to which an enormous amount of thought, concern and devotion had been given, it was observed and studied by other branches of the medical profession as well. It was realized that the development of medicine and surgery, together with advanced equipment and modern drugs and techniques, were not sufficient to heal local patients. Particularly for treatments which lasted for longer periods, the surroundings in which the patients were kept and

227

treated were important factors for healing. Thus my work on hospitals and medical institutions, especially those in rural areas, grew.

In out-of-the-way districts, among the scattered and neglected population, the buildings needed were small, but whatever the size they were essential necessities—more essential and necessary than even those in the densely-populated cities where plenty of alternative facilities are available. Furthermore, those living in these remote rural areas traded by the barter system rather than by buying and selling with money. This meant that it was extremely difficult to find money to pay for the building material, and so it was of the utmost importance to design and make buildings that were strong and durable, and as inexpensive as possible. For this and other similar reasons I became very cost-conscious and spent a lot of time trying to find ways of reducing building costs in general—whether I was using local indigenous methods or building with the 'normal' twentieth century materials and techniques. Seeing millions of people living a hand-to-mouth existence made me come to abhor all forms of extravagance and waste.

This brings us to the two important characteristics of a so-called Baker Architecture—that 'small' is not only 'beautiful' but is often essential and even more important than 'large'; and that if we architects are even to start coping effectively with the real building problems and the housing needs of the world, we must learn how to build as inexpensively as possible.

And so my interest and work spread. The medical world was cautiously interested and the world of formal education also started to nibble at Baker's baits. There were village schools and colleges and even urban colleges who wanted libraries, auditoria, etc. Designing for these various institutions became my bread-and-butter. For the dessert I could never resist the invitation to design religious buildings. So, often, there were *ashrams*, houses of prayer and churches on my drawing board—but always on the condition that there must be no ostentation or 'façade-ism'. I am often puzzled by the dichotomy in my nature—I claim to believe in democracy but I can find myself wanting to be an achitectural dictator! I think I am more than normally tolerant about other people's religious beliefs and practices, and yet I can find myself decrying the requests of a religious group for something which I feel is wrong or inconsistent with their beliefs. I claim that the client's needs and desires should come first and that he requires a 'client-based' building, not a 'Baker' building—but when expressions of his religious beliefs offend me I find myself unable to design for him.

Very briefly, the Quaker ideal is that there is a form of direct unity with the Creator, that Man experiences this at any time, in any place and under any circumstances. Special 'religious' surroundings and appurtenances are not essential, though many people find them a help. But, however much we hoodwink our fellowmen, it is impossible to be deceitful or put up a false front to the Creator. So all efforts to 'put on a big show' or indulge in deceit to make ourselves look greater than we are, seems to be quite pointless. A house has to be designed as a home for a particular group of people to live together as a family in their own inimitable style and if this planning and designing for them is done well it is highly unlikely that the outside of the building will be ostentatious or showy. It is even more so with religious buildings where people usually gather together for purposes of worship and prayer, with their own particular form of ritual or liturgy. The architect will do his utmost to provide the 'right' space in which these acts of worship can be made. As this mainly concerns our search for union with the Eternal it seems particularly 'not right' to indulge in a pretentious façade with these buildings. This anti-façade-ism has definitely been a very noticeable and is a deliberate characteristic of Laurie Baker's architecture, no matter what type of building is being designed.

It was towards the end of our stay in Pithoragarh and while these interesting, special buildings were being built that the government itself started mild enquiries, especially concerning the possibilities of cost-reduction in building. Senior government secretaries showed genuine concern at architectural practices which were apparently not actually essential or even desirable, but which they were assured were necessary. At first I was only unofficially asked whether there were in fact any possible ways of reducing costs for government buildings done by government agencies. My unpopularity among fellow professionals probably started at this time. I remember being shown drawings of a monumental façade to the proposed State Archival Buildings. The entrance portico looked very much like St. Paul's Cathedral West Facade with a huge flight of steps and rows of ornate columns. The public would not use this building and those who were to work in it would number less than forty. I asked for the reason for the great entrance portico the answer I received was that it was because Mr Nehru himself would declare the building open! Needless to say I enjoyed these skirmishes with the government personnel and eventually became an official adviser.

For a number of a reasons we pulled up our roots from our Himalayan home and moved south to the State of Kerala with its extremely beautiful local indigenous bamboo style of architecture. Again, at first, we chose a remoter rural area to live and work in, and again, we ourselves built our own home and hospital in the local style with local materials. We settled down to live in a completely different setting from that of north India. I found the relationships of Kerala to India very comparable to that of Britain to the rest of Europe. The people were 'insular' and proud, and their ways were very different (and in their own eyes superior) to those of others. Many more people were educated and literate, and this was especially true among the women folk. This had both advantages and disadvantages. For example, there were many very attractive ways of using local building materials. The coconut palm leaf was split and the fronds plaited together to form a thatch which was pleasing to the eye and of extremely good insulation value. The plaiting work had always been done by the older girls in their spare time, but now almost all girls went to school and more and more of them to college and there was neither the time nor the inclination to make these stocks of thatched leaves ready for the annual re-thatching. And so, for similar reasons, there was a strong move everywhere to abandon 'old-fashioned ways' and go in for 'modern' buildings using plenty of cement and reinforced concrete.

I had little time for the usual sharing of my wife's hospital work as I became more and more involved in building activities. Many people and institutions showed great interest in reducing costs of building. It all started when the Kerala Bishops' conference had tried to find a way of working together for the good of the common poor man. They had, with great fanfare, agreed that each parish in the state should try and put up at least one inexpensive, small house and give it to the poorest family in that parish, regardless of caste or creed. But after three years only two or three houses had been built. The Archbishop Mar Gregorios of Trivandrum called for a 'post-mortem' seminar to find out the reason for this failure. The explanation given by all was simple enough—there was no longer any such thing as an 'inexpensive building'! I offered to demonstrate, rather than to talk about ways of building inexpensive houses and spent the following two weeks putting up a small house of about forty square metres and costing, by request, less than Rs 3,000 (about US $400). The participants of the conference came to see the result of this demonstration and to our amazement declared the house to be 'too good' for 'the poor'. So the Archbishop asked for a second house to be put up for half the cost.

From this beginning there followed many small houses, schools, clinics, hospitals and churches and then the government moved in to examine what was going on. The Chief Minister of the state became a convert and I built the State Institute of Languages, at his request, for a small sum of money which the Works and Housing Department had declared was impossible. But my work for government and semi-government institutions continued, notably with a fairly large and prestigious complex known as the Centre for Development Studies, staffed and run by world-known economists of repute. The Chief Minister launched the scheme by challenging them to demonstrate and prove their economic theories by the way in which they built and ran their institution.

At this time, my greatest problems came from the vested interests of most categories of people concerned with the building industry. Most of them were paid on a percentage basis of the total or partial cost of a building. Clearly they did not wish to reduce costs! The craftsmen also were similarly paid and they too did not want any changes. It became increasingly tiresome when people who asked me to design a building for them for a certain sum of money, would return to say that the builders said it could not be done even for double the figure I had given. There was only one thing to do and that was to get together a band of masons and carpenters who would do what was asked of them and who would learn new techniques and un-learn old, wasteful ones. It was rewarding for my clients, for me and for the workmen. For example, some of them became excellent brick-workers who got enormous satisfaction from producing beautiful brickwork. Much of what has come to be described as Baker Architecture I owe to these craftsmen. Because of them it became easy for me to construct almost any type of building, and these ranged from the smallest houses to a large cathedral seating three thousand people. I was particularly pleased that three housing groups were taking advantage of these ideas. A whole fishing village, for example, was built after many of its old huts had been washed away by the sea in a gale. Several institutions also built houses for their poor at comparatively very little cost. Then the so-called 'upper strata' of society came forward with interest which proved to be genuine, when quite a lot of them asked me to build their houses for them using these simple, cost-reducing techniques.

Low-cost housing techniques were the most rewarding for the group of people who came under the label of the 'lower middle class'. They feel they have certain standards of living to keep up, matters relating to dress and to the education and marriage of their children, but their salaries leave them very little to save for house-building—an activity which they had always considered well beyond their reach. Now they could build. They were quick to understand the principles involved in cost-reduction. They were quick to understand the real priorities of building a home. They had and expressed their faith in the 'expert', and would sometimes actually help where they felt they could.

Again the government showed further interest and called for a report on the methods of cost-reduction. There was strong opposition to the idea of requesting a private individual with 'funny' ideas to present an official report to the government. Three outside government experts joined me and the report was presented, and, accepted, after the Chief Minister had organized a seminar in which all the suggestions and recommendations in the report were thrashed out and either agreed upon as possible and feasible, or, if impossible, rejected. Finally everything in the report was accepted, but over the years very little of it has been implemented.

Industrialists are often hard realists and the principles of cost-reduction have been taken up by some of them in different parts of the country. It seems a far cry from small 'low-cost houses' to big foundries and factories, but that is what has happened. The wheel seems to have turned a full circle because it is these indusrialists who are now employing many handicapped persons and my work for the industrialists includes hostels and training-centres for these handicapped people, along with their huge factory buildings.

Lastly, I have found, consistently, throughout my working life, that the whole business of planning and designing is intensely absorbing *and* fun! Always living close to nature I learnt many lessons from the design of God's creations. Very rarely do we find the square or the rectangle but very often the circle is used. The straight line is rare, but the graceful curve is frequently seen. An interesting scientific observation is that the length of the wall enclosing a given area is shorter if the shape is circular and longer if the shape around the same area is a square or a rectangle. This is an important factor in cost-reducing excercises! Furthermore, I have found the answer to many spatial and planning problems by using the circle and the curve instead of the square and the straight line—and building becomes much more fun with the circle.

(unpublished)

Building Technology in Pithoragarh

The prime concern in the paper is with the lives of the people who live in the remoter and more scattered communities of the mountain district of Pithoragarh. I lived near Pithoragarh in the 1940s when there were no motor roads. Scattered villages and hamlets were linked to each other only by narrow tracks which ran either along the contours of mountains or climbed up from river to mountain-pass and then down again to the next river. My wife was a doctor and, although our hospital was nearby, we had to travel widely to visit patients who were too ill to be brought over difficult mountain paths to the hospital. We therefore got to know the countryside well and, more especially, the ways of living of the people with whom we lived and whom we treated. As an architect, I was always also extremely interested in their building constructions and the functional way in which they planned their homes.

One of the things that Mahatma Gandhi had said, that impressed me, and has influenced my thinking more than anything else, was that the ideal houses in the ideal village will be built of materials which are all found within a five-mile radius of the house. In my training as an architect, I have seen clearly wonderful examples of Gandhiji's wisdom all around me. The wood for the roofs was obtained locally and was extravagantly lavish in size. Whole tree-trunks were used for ridge-poles, purlins and trusses. A layer of split-pine was laid over thick rafters and carried the split-stone or slate-roofing which was bedded in mud. All these roofing materials were close at hand. Occasionally a wealthier person would send for a thinner quality of slate a few miles away. This whole roof construction over the wall construction was completely adequate to cope with the climatic extremes of heat and dryness in summer, the violent rainstorms in monsoons and the heavy snow in winter.

In planning, the houses were similarly simple and functional. Almost invariably they were built along the side of a steeply sloping hill or mountainside. So split-levels were very common. Unnecessary excavation was avoided. On the outer lower side was the *ghot*—cellar-like rooms with only one outer wall which was full of doors and windows. Usually the *ghot* was occupied by the cattle; sometimes part of it was also used as the kitchen; and there were, sometimes, store rooms down below. On the next half-level up, but on the opposite and sunny side, was the lean-to veranda, with its low door and its low balcony-like arched carved windows with wooden shutters. Here was the main entrance to the house and it was also the entertaining and the sitting part of the house. One could sit in the winter light coming in at a low angle, or in summer, when one got the breeze and the shade to keep cool and fresh in the sultry summer heat. At night the shutters were fastened and the low-roofed room quickly warmed up as the family sat around the *angeethi*. On the third split level, above the animal *ghot*, were the private, square, dark rooms—they were a mixture of bedroom and store room. Often even the cooking and eating took place in one of these inner rooms which gained added warmth and heat from the animals below.

Village planning and site utilization were equally functional and simple. Usually there were rows of houses all joined together (sometimes, when three to ten or twelve brothers with their families lived in such a row of houses the front veranda was common to all). These multi-housed rows of dwellings were usually under one big long common roof. The rows followed the contours wherever possible, and, consequently, were sometimes curved. The row of houses was usually sited to overlook the terraced fields below, to catch the sunshine, and to get protection from rain, snow and cold winds from the forest or the steep hillside behind and above the row.

To me, this Himalayan domestic architecture was a perfect example of vernacular architecture—simple, efficient, inexpensive. This delightful dignified housing demonstrated hundreds of years of building research on coping with local materials, using them to cope with the local climatic patterns and hazards, and accommodating to the local social pattern of living. It dealt with incidental difficult problems of building on a steeply sloping site, coping with earthquakes and avoiding landsliding areas and paths. The few examples of attempts to 'modernize' housing merely demonstrated, only too clearly and adequately, our modern conceit and showed how very foolish we are when we attempt to ignore or abandon the hundreds of years of 'research' that goes into local building methods.

But what do the people who still live in the Pithoragarh district think of their actual housing needs?

I want to know what the inhabitants think of their own houses. Some of you may come originally from Pithoragarh—but now you have become urbanized in Nainital or Bareilly or Lucknow or even Delhi. You will be suggesting proper kitchens, bathrooms, latrines, chimneys, smokeless *chulhas*, glass windows, brick walls, concrete floors and roofs and so on. But my experience has shown that such 'improvements' create problems worse than those which they are supposed to remedy, and that they are rarely appreciated by the people who have to live with these 'advancements' and 'developments'.

Quite frankly, I wish to question whether there is an actual housing need in the outlying villages?

If there is any express need for more housing in the remoter areas, then what are the current problems and difficulties in building the normal traditional type of house?

Almost certainly there will be complaints about the rise of prices, particularly of labour and timber. The rise in labour-costs is something that has come to stay and there is little that we can do about it. In Pithoragarh, almost all the costs of a building were labour-costs. Stone, for example, lay on the ground next to the house site—the entire cost of producing stone lumps, ready to assemble, was one of labour. It involved levering out the layers of stone and carrying them as head-load to the masons building the walls. This is in contrast to the brick areas where, besides labour, there are several other manufacturing and transport costs involved. The other big problem is timber. There has been a lot of timber-felling, particularly uncontrolled felling of privately-owned timber, which has not been replaced by new planting. In the state forests there was always proper control of felling, but now that the country is aware of the value of timber and of the fact that these forests are not limitless (but have a definite measurable content which has decreased drastically over the last quarter of a century), timber has joined the rank of luxury items and so we can no longer afford to use it lavishly.

236

We also have to remember that there will be other modifications with regard to planning and details of services. These will be related to other problems, such as the increasing problem of fuel. Till now, of course, all cooking fuel, and even most of the lighting fuel came from the forests. This has now been curbed and other fuels are being used—this is bound to have an effect on housing.

It is an accumulation of all these various changes that makes the old 'deal' (Gandhian!) sort of village house inadequate and deficient. It is essential for us to decide what we actually mean by these currently fashionable terms—'intermediate', 'appropriate' or 'adaptive' technologies! My own interpretation is that these technologies are those which show us the easiest, simplest, least-expensive but efficient ways of dealing with everyday problems. Such technologies are affordable, as the commodities required are easily available and so are the skills needed for the job. My observation is that vernacular architecture almost always has apt solutions to all our problems of building. All that is required is to go a step further with the research our forefathers have done—that is, to *add on* our twentieth century experience to *improve on* what has already been accomplished. But this addition should be a contribution—not a contradiction.

Science and Rural Development in Mountains
(edited by J.S. Singh, S.P. Singh and C. Shastri,
Gyandoya Prakashan, Nainital, 1980)

Architectural Anarchy

People who come to Kerala almost invariably express delight in its architectural styles. Until a few years ago each town had its own distinctive character. There are many factors which contribute to this character-formation. One relates to town-planning. Old towns usually started as very small settlements and slowly grew into towns. This meant that often there was no road system to begin with and it only came slowly as the need to communicate with other places arose. Even then, the roads meandered to avoid hazards and natural features such as hills and rocks, trees and water, or old religious buildings that they felt should not be moved. So right from the start every location itself determined the original basic layout.

The other factor is related to the construction of buildings. Before these days of easy, but costly, transport, people built only with the materials that were found nearby. For example, you would not find any buildings of burnt brick in an area of rock and stone. As the local materials varied from place to place, so did the appearance of the building constructed with them. The variation was found not only in colour and texture and but also in the shape and/or height of the building. The materials also determined the shape and size of the holes in walls for the doors and windows.

An important factor in determining the character of a town is the living patterns and social habits of the people who inhabit it. Each community and settlement evolves its own special pattern of living, its own idea of culture and religion. Indeed, architecture is the way in which groups and communities use local materials to construct buildings which will cope with the local hazards, natural features, climatic conditions and cultural, social and religious patterns.

Some special features are obvious in the buildings of old villages, towns and cities of India. The first is the simple, straightforward, honest way of using local materials. For instance, in areas where the local stone,

238

is smooth and sleek, such as marble, the builders have exploited the characteristics of the stone resulting in smooth and elegant buildings. Where forests abounded, buildings made use of wood. But as there are many types of timber, there are different ways of using wood of different kinds. All this is fairly obvious, but the point I want to make is summed up in the word I have used to describe the use of materials—the word 'honest'. Put simply, it means that a brick wall looks like a brick wall and you could, if you so choose, count the number of bricks on it. A stone wall makes use of the sparkling quality of granite or the rich colour of standstone.

Another result of this honest use of local materials is that the architecture is not confined to the main buildings but integrates, in its design, all of the immediate surroundings, such as walls, gates, seats, water features like fountains, posts for lights, paths, paving and steps.

The factors I have mentioned so far give a unique harmony and unity to each old town. But there is another major factor of design that forms the character of towns—the factor of scale. This means that all the details in a building are related to the size of the human figure. We know that the height of most adults is between five and six feet. When we look at the façade of a building and see a door in it, we know that it is a little higher than ourselves, that it is probably between six and seven feet. In this way, without measuring or calculating, we can roughly judge the size of buildings and rooms by merely looking at the door. Of course, there are exceptions, as the entrances to special buildings such as temples and churches. These often have large doors for ceremonial purposes through which banners are carried and elephants pass. In these cases the scale of the building is lost unless there is also an ordinary door somewhere. The question of scale was obviously understood by our forefathers and has proved to be another strong unifying factor in determining the character of a town and its domestic architecture. Furthermore, this adherence to scale provides a harmony and unity between buildings of different ages. In most of the old towns some buildings may be hundreds of years older than others and while systems and techniques of building construction slowly changed through the centuries, the continuity, harmony and unity was maintained by the use of the same materials, the use of scale and a continuous relationship with the size of the human figure.

All that I have said applies particularly to the various styles of architecture in Kerala. Local materials have been used simply and honestly. One can see what the foundation is built of, what materials are used for the superstructure; and the details of the beautiful roof timbers cleverly designed to carry tiles or thatch. The scale is consistent and, again, honest.

In Japan, China and Korea, the original basic style stemmed from the use of bamboo. Bamboo is long and flexible—rarely straight, but usually gracefully curving. This is particularly expressed when it is used as the roof's ridge pole, carried between two forked poles. It sags in the middle and soars upwards, at the ends, beyond the points of support. With the development of tools, bamboo-workers graduated to carpenters and the wood they used was often from palms and tended to curve gracefully. Kerala has a hot, wet, humid, tropical climate, so the roof pitch is steep and the eaves come down low to protect the walls from heavy rain and, at other times of the year, from hot strong sunlight. Rooms in the houses were mainly used for storage and for brief periods of privacy, and were therefore small. Deep, shady, cool verandas were used for living purposes. There was very little difference in urban and rural buildings.

But what have we done in the second half of the twentieth century? Is there any new town in Kerala, or any new part of a town in Kerala which is now worth going to see for its strength of character or beauty? If there is, I have missed it. All that one can see today is a growing hotch-potch of many-storeyed buildings in the so-called 'modern' style. Rarely is any natural material, whether local or imported, visible. All structural elements—mainly reinforced concrete frames with fewer load-bearing walls—are hidden or clad with cement plaster, paint, glass, aluminium and such like. Scale has been completely abandoned. There are pointless and functionless protrusions, frills and fins that have little or no relation to the rooms and their functions. Façadism, a thing unknown in the traditional Kerala architecture, is rife and it is here that the scaleless fins proliferate. Each separate building is an expression of anarchy with no thought of harmony, unity or honesty with itself, let alone with its neighbours or with the environment.

The contemporary approach seems to be towards an architectural anarchy of ruthless arrogance. Instead of the harmonious, honest, traditional architecture of Kerala, we now seem to prefer a senseless jumble of high-rise concrete structures, each unit clad in the most unsuitable materials we can think of. The scene is of strife, division, violence and communalism. Perhaps we are merely reflecting the present-day social milieu of strife, divisions, violence and communalism in our architecture. In being modern, virtue has gone.

The India Magazine
August 1984

241

Is a Modern Indian Architecture Possible?

In most countries of the world architects are being accused of failing to produce a modern form of their own previously-distinctive architectural styles. If one or two typical modern buildings from each country could be transported and put down in isolation in a large flat desert, could any of us, even architects, walk from one building to another and say 'Ah! A modern Fijian masterpiece' and 'Wow! Just look at this one—pure Italian' and further on 'My! This is obviously an Indian effort!' A hundred or so years ago we could probably have been successful with such identifications, but there are very grave doubts whether we can do so now.

Does this mean that we have failed in our job?

Fifty years ago we were taught that a building must have an identity. We could certainly tell by looking at a building whether it was domestic or commercial or industrial and so on. It also had its geographical and cultural characteristics. In India there is an incredible wealth of regional architectural styles, and there is not the faintest possibility of confusing one with another. Even where the same materials have been used for building, the climatic, cultural and regional variations are so great that different methods of construction have been used to produce unique individual styles. Further, these distinctive styles apply not only to big and important buildings but also to the smallest domestic structures. Really we can say that the buildings of any small district are a quintessence of that district's culture and skill.

But these distinctions cannot be found anymore. What has happened?

For one thing—cement. Modern Portland cement came and suddenly our slow, steady, evolutionary building process came to a devastating and tragic halt. Cement and steel were joined in holy matrimony and lo!—their child was this universal anonymous expressionless 'modern architecture' which tells you nothing except that reinforced concrete has been lavishly and brutally used. The saddest thing about it is that reinforced concrete is a wonderful material that can do almost everything fantastic and exciting. It can stand, soar, twist, hang, swirl, gyrate, encircle, defy and placate. But we rarely ever let it do any of these exciting things. We merely imitate the building practices of the Dravidians, with their square stone pillars and split stone beams; and when in a very dare-devil mood we cantilever out the beam-ends to an uncomfortable length, we think we are really and truly 'modern'.

Of course, we have a third deadly material, glass—with which we fill in all the holes. The result of this modern but static style of architecture, is that everybody's buildings, be they in Bombay, Birmingham, Bologna or Buenos Aires, look the same.

Consolingly, 'high technology' has also taught us that there is no need to concern ourselves with the weather or the functions for which the building will be used, or the variations in the cultural patterns of our clients—'high technology' applique-work can cope with all this old-fashioned 'nonsense'.

I think the time has come to ask ourselves a lot of questions. Could we have done something different? Should we have done something different? What does 'modern' mean? Can't we be 'modern' with other materials besides reinforced concrete, glass and aluminium trimmings? Can't we go back to the year 1 BC (Before Concrete) and carry on with that wonderful history of research and development by applying twentieth century knowledge and know-how while still showing love and respect for all that has gone before us?

Perhaps speed has been one of the major contributing factors leading to that catastrophic break with tradition. It probably took a thousand years for us to find out by trial-and-error how to make a mud wall impervious to rain and wind, another thousand years to learn how to keep termites out of it and another two or three thousand to learn how to build multi-storeyed mud buildings. But we did do it, and our enemies on the other side of the hill also did it, though in their own way which was different from ours. Now 'developed communications' has taken the 'wonder material' to all the corners of the earth and we have

243

succumbed to it like children falling upon a dish of instant hot cakes. So we all have identical pot-bellies and have forgotten 'mother's cooking'. Fortunately, the rebellion against 'instant mixes' has already begun and there is a yearning for 'fresh-compost-fed-vegetables and wholemeal-bread'—so may be there is hope that we too as architects, can, as our road signs say, 'Stop! Look! Proceed!'

In view of the fact that there are over twenty million families in India without any sort of shelter, that we have to import cement from Korea to make up for the shortfalls, that we are using up a lot of our energy resources at an alarming rate, and that we have bred some of the top brains in the world of science, we should, for instance, in areas where mud has been the traditional staple building material, show how modern we can be with mud! Where burnt brick has been the main building material can't we produce bricks with less energy and use them in a modern way? There are experiments which show that this sort of thing can be done along with the new wonder materials to produce buildings that are 'modern', beautiful, characterful and identifiable with a particular region and its people. For example, in the State of Kerala there is high rainfall, strong winds, powerful tropical sun and a lot of humidity. The result of ancient research and development work was a steeply-pitched roof which threw off torrential continuous rains and protected walls and rooms from the glare and heat of the sun. It all made good sense and good architecture. But concrete and glass towers are incredibly expensive because of all the antics required to cope with rain and sun, and they are quite stupidly useless without the air-conditioners, fans and louvres of aluminium strips. Can 'modern' architecture only be vertical of wall and flat of roof? Couldn't we throw off rain and protect from sun *and* show that we are doing it effectively, even by being 'modern'?

Since the beginning of recorded art, India's brains had devised the *jali* (trellis, lattice, honey-combed walling, pierced stone and wooden screens and walls) to filter the glare and strong sunlight into cool but breeze-filled rooms. India has used this device more than any other country and it is essentially an Indian device. We can study the many and varied components of Indian architectural design and find out what makes them essentially and intriguingly 'Indian'. Only then can we

create an Indian-ness into all our materials and designing. *Then* our
'modern' 'Indian' architecture will be a continuing, growing, crowning
glory to our great heritage.

Spazio Societa
Milan, 1986

Architecture and the People

The theme of this essay is Architectural Awareness. The dictionary defines 'awareness' as being conscious, alert and mentally responsive to something. Architecture is the style and method of design and construction of buildings or the art and science of building. So our subject is about our consciousness, alertness and mental response to the art and design and construction of buildings.

The subject given to me is 'Architecture and the People'. Did the promoters mean *the people*, or could they have said 'Architecture and People'? Saying 'the People' implies that we architects are in one category and *the people* in another. It sounds a bit like royalty talking about 'my people'—implying a large conglomeration of lesser mortals. So for the sake of this discussion I will accept this title of 'Architecture and the People', and put myself in the position of the architect looking at all my clients (who are supposed to know nothing about architecture) and the millions of people who have no option but to look at and accept 'our' architecture.

But what do architects and what do the people have in their minds when they hear the word 'Architecture'? I unobtrusively tried to find out what the people think—and found that a very large proportion, especially architects, think of the word with a capital 'A' and feel that it mainly applies to 'proper, big, important buildings'. In fact for most of us and for the people the word architecture would be immediately associated with something as grand and magnificient as the Taj Mahal of Agra. So, not surprisingly, when I am wandering through a village or an old town, entranced and fascinated by the old buildings and happen to make some such remark as 'what fascinating architecture', there is a tendency to get a response as 'where?'—because there is no temple or town-hall or tower in sight, but only thatched and tiled houses and shops.

246

This indicates that we are on different wavelengths, even about our own profession and what it means to us. So I appeal to all to have an open mind when we listen to each others ideas!

From the many years of experience in Pithoragarh and Trivandrum I learnt what Indian architecture is. I did not learn it from books or from architects, but from ordinary village craftsmen, carpenters, masons, mud-workers, thatchers—in other words from ordinary people, *the people!*

When I first moved to India, my headquarters were in Fyzabad in the state of Uttar Pradesh. How could I build and design for the extremes of climate found here? At times we were freezing and at other times the temperature went up to 115° F. At times it would rain cats and dogs and at other times the ground was so dry—like concrete with a layer of dust over it. When the sun beat down after the monsoons, it was like being in a steambath; when the *loo* (hot winds) blew, everything we ate would be gritty and sandy. The following week I would be in Bihar, or Kerala, or Maharashtra or Orissa—every place having its own climate. In some places the land was all sand, other places had reclaimed backwaters and swamps, and in yet others, laterite and black cotton soil were found.

Another impression, of the local traditional architecture, that was formed as years of designing and building went by and as I travelled and worked over the country with the enormous variation in materials, construction techniques, and design, was that the quality of architecture did not depend upon the size or significance ('importance') of the building. Most huts had admirable and delightful proportions and shapes. There was an incredible honesty and a strong aspect of truth in all the indigenous buildings. Mud looked like mud, but its application was well-controlled and often the hand-work marks gave decoration and scale to the walls. Mud was never made to look like some 'superior' material. Brick also looked like brick, and, again, ingenious patterns often gave beauty and scale to the buildings. Rough stone was not smeared over with plaster or some such covering material—it looked rugged, strong and stone-like. Timber-work had a wonderfully rich variety of joints and finishes. The people relied on the honest use of materials. Thus all the answers to my problems came from *the people*. I continue to be amazed and thrilled at the practical knowledge, principles and skills which *the people* have.

During this period I lived and moved through a wide range of cultures and religions. The caste and community feelings were still very prevalent. On the trains there was Hindu *pani*, and there was Muslim *cha*! People not only had inherited building and planning principles but they also had superstitions passed down to them. I was told that the grinding stone in the kitchen must not look at the fire, that the occupants must not open the front door and look to the south, that the kitchen must face a certain direction. At first I rebelled against these—but slowly I found that although these quaint notions looked like superstitions, since the people could not give me an explanation, more often than not there was a rationale behind them.

This experience led me to realize that the architect is only an 'extra' to the total architecture of our country. Many will probably think that this is sentimental rubbish—but I can only direct you to study the National Census, or to walk with your eyes open through any village, town or city, and you will see that it is unlikely that we architects have had anything at all to do with more than 0.001 per cent of the total number of buildings in the country, and that much of our indigenous architecture is of a high quality of design.

I am now convinced that good or bad design, or good or bad taste has little to do with colour, or form, or texture, or costliness—but that it has only to do with honesty and truth in the choice of materials and the method of using them.

I have had the pleasure and the privilege of living and working with various remote communities and tribal groups—each with their own distinctive architecture and all with the simple, honest use of materials. I am continually amazed at the care taken in simple effective detailing. Beautiful doors without hinges, strong effective valleys and gutters in roofing, unorthodox but good bonding. They also know how to improvize and adapt to make the buildings more efficient and the living conditions easier. In Andhra, there are energy-efficient *chulhas* made from broken water-pots. In Tamil Nadu, old cow's horns are embedded into the wall as a clothes-hanger. All over the country a variety of ingenious and decorative shelves and recesses are found in thick walls, and sleeping and storage lofts above the lintel level. All this shows a mastery of a three-dimensional approach to the use of space.

The following are my conclusions from a lifetime of building with *the people*.

> *First:* I have never had any personal doubts about who my real clients are. They have never been to me categories—'tribals', 'fishermen' 'HIG' or 'EWS'. They have been people with names and with personalities.
>
> *Second:* I have never doubted that in a country like ours any of us has any right to squander or waste, or use unnecessarily, money, materials or energy.
>
> *Third:* After my first few months in India I never doubted the inherent and inherited ability of *the people* to know what good architecture is. With limited resources they have built for themselves effectively and well; and we can learn from them!
>
> *Fourth:* Personally, I am not happy designing buildings by sitting in isolation at a desk in an office. My designing comes into my head while I am with the clients on their site—and I believe, like *the people*, in improvization and alteration, as the work proceeds.

To conclude, almost certainly your ideas and mine of what an architect should be, are likely to be very different. Probably you are right—but I have no regrets about the ideas I have formed and the training I have had during the past forty-eight years from *the people*! Unfortunately, their inherited skills and knowledge are now being forgotten, lost and ignored. I think it is up to us to try and keep them alive by helping them improve on what their parents have passed on to them, to accommodate for the constantly changing and increasing needs as their numbers grow.

(unpublished)

The Industrial Designer and Housing

My work is entirely connected with providing shelter for people to live and work in. My field is a wide one and I am often asked to help solve the building problems in different parts of India. The requests come from all strata of society.

India has over six hundred million people and over three hundred million of them have to try and live on less than one rupee per person per day. Over twenty million Indian families have nothing that can be described as a house to live in. The urban dweller needs shelter, but to free himself from slum conditions he must also have an approach to his home, and he must have water and light and power, and there must be adequate drainage and sanitation facilities. The rural family also needs, in addition, shelter, water, drainage and security for his livestock, hens, goats, pigs or cows which this is all a part of his 'home'.

Having tried to understand the housing needs of the people of India, I must try and think what sort of a building I can design for the average Indian to live in. But who is an 'average Indian'? I have to remember that he lives in rural surroundings (about eighty- five per cent of the population is rural) and is occupied with work for only seven months of the year. When he has shared the money that he earns in one year with his family dependents, he has less than one rupee per day to spend on all the things he needs for a living. He is labelled as 'unskilled'. Though this means that he is unskilled in wage-earning jobs, I personally believe that he is actually very skilled in the many small ways which make life possible for him.

So, to solve the problem of housing, I must concern myself with this 'average Indian'. He himself cannot, and does not, commission me to design for him. I receive my orders and instructions from the government and other institutions. But I would be a wicked blind fool if I design only for those who can afford to commission my services as an architect. Is it not possible to remain realistic and design for the 'have nots'?

I believe it possible, but I desperately need the help of industrial designers. The picture of need is not so desperate as mere statistical figures indicate. India is a vast country nearly two thousand miles wide and two thousand miles from top to bottom. Man, all over India, has shown in his vernacular styles of domestic architecture that he can make use of the locally-available, plentiful, simple, inexpensive materials immediately around him to protect himself from the weather—from rain and snow, heat and cold, strong winds, cyclones and floods. He has shown how he can use them to fit in with cultural and community pattern of living and how he can use them to protect himself from other men, wild beasts and animals, reptiles and insects. In such a vast country as India we therefore have hundreds of these vernacular styles which sometimes vary within every few miles—if slightly, but very significantly. So as an architect, and with you as industrial designers, we have a solid strong efficient spring-board from which we can launch our attack on the problems of the 'average Indian' for his housing.

Now let us look at the many component parts of the building.

We need foundations which carry our buildings on soils that are often poor and uncooperative—such as black cotton soils, loose sands, soils that are ever rich in organic matter, soils that are waterlogged. Usually, the vernacular style copes with this problem but we must see whether we can add on to the solution of these foundation problems. At present I am experimenting with surface ring-beam foundations using very simple and crude concrete reinforced with materials such as bamboo.

Above the foundations are walls which must stand up for a lifetime. They must not crumble or erode or provide homes for reptiles, insects or termites. They must not need too much maintenance or frequent replacement. There are many traditional methods of building walls. Can we, with the twentieth century know-how, make any improvements or reduction of cost without reducing their strength and durability? I have confined myself to the use of traditional materials, but I find I am able to improvize on some of them, for instance with improved stabilizers of soil so that walls are termite-free or fire-resistant.

251

The walls are pierced by openings with doors and windows. Doors should be strong and protective. Windows have many functions and every window need not necessarily cope with every function. So we often *over*-design them. They are often far more elaborate and therefore more expensive than needed. The many functions a window serves are: to look out of, to let in light, air, or to let in light but keep out wind and rain, or to do all of these things but remain protective and provide security, or perhaps to perform different functions at different times.

The roofs give protection from rain, wind, heat and cold and at the same time provide security. Again, I have mainly used traditional materials and units; but often the cost can be reduced by using materials in different ways, or by introducing a system common to one area another area where similar materials are to be found. For example, often people clamour for solid concrete roof slabs for security, long life, and resistance from fire, but these are far too expensive. I have used waste Mangalore tiles, or clay pots, or forms of hollow or light-weight bricks as fillers in a grid-slab system. This reduces cost and improves insulation.

Floors must wear well, not crack, and be easy to clean. They should not let moisture and cold rise from the earth beneath. I have tried simplified mosaic systems and have also tried to re-introduce various forms of old-fashioned country clay flooring tiles. I have tried long and hard to persuade tile manufacturers to give us simple, strong, inexpensive flooring tiles using salt or load glasses, but they say people will not use them. People say nobody offers them to us except at exorbitant costs. And again surely there are possibilities from the use of waste materials? The green coating of the coconut shells have been used to make hardboards by hot-press methods. This could be developed as a cheap, strong flooring material.

Sanitation is often lacking in our homes mainly because the currently-available devices are intricate, poorly-designed and very expensive. The ordinary wash-basin, for example, is a shocking corruption of the nineteenth century European device of their ideas of sanitation and cleaning. It is *not* convenient or suited to Indian needs; and yet, as an architect, I have no option but to use these outmoded Victorian contraptions.

People need cooked food and most cooking devices are still primitive and thereby removed from the three stones to support a pot over a fire of wooden twigs. But all refinements and developments are expensive and beyond the reach of the average purse. Fuel has become scarce and expensive. Non-conventional energy devices like the biogas plants and solar cookers are beyond the reach of the average Indian because of their forbidding cost. And industrial designers do not realize that the people who are most in need of economical cooking facilities are those three hundred million people who have to try and survive on one rupee a day.

People living in hot tropical regions do not need stuffed, heat-retaining furniture for sitting and sleeping on. Most traditional sitting and sleeping devices were built in as part of the structure. But nowadays such a system only adds to the building cost unless very carefully planned. What simple, inexpensive furniture are we designing? Can we use more multi-purpose units and can they be designed as house-structural elements too?

A man needing a house would turn to builders and artisans to convert his materials into a house to live in. But where are our new building shops? Why can't we go to a building shop and pick out the doors and windows we need; the ventilators, cupboards, kitchen and cooking devices, bathroom and sanitary units, floor and roof and walling panels or blocks, lighting and furniture fixtures which we think will suit our tastes and our purses? We find a few of these things scattered and isolated, but usually poorly designed and terribly expensive and certainly beyond the reach of our 'average Indian'.

The scope to stock 'building shops' with everything a man needs to put his home together is simply enormous. Architects, engineers and building contractors merely express the needs of the people.

Paper presented at a seminar on 'Design for Development'
(organized by the United Nations Industrial Development
Organization (UNIDO), at the National Institute of Design (NID),
Ahmedabad, January 1979)

Does Cost-Reduction Mean Poor Quality?

A look at the overall picture of the present building industry makes it clear that the cost of building is extremely high and well beyond the means of the ordinary man. There are drastic shortages of what we regard as essential building materials. There are ever-increasing labour problems and we get less and less return in skill and quality of work for higher and higher wages.

It seems likely that if these trends persist the building industry will almost cease to exist. Or else we must go through some form of revolution whose battlecry should be 'reduce costs, without a corresponding reduction in standards of quality'.

But what can be done to reduce building costs? I think we have to ask ourselves whether we really do require many of the expensive buildings that are springing up all round us. The example I have in mind concerns Kerala's housing needs. We have a State Housing Board to cope with this problem—but it must have spent several lakhs on its own seven-storey office block which has no housing in it but overlooks Trivandrum's biggest slum in which thousands of people live in squalor.

In almost all institutional buildings we find rooms with such labels as 'Board Room', 'Conference Hall', 'Seminar Room', 'Exhibition Hall', and so on. Probably all these rooms are necessary but very often they lie idle and unused except for brief periods of usage. Multi-use planning could possibly save on quantity and building cost could be reduced.

Another example of such planning in quantity is found in school buildings. In many parts of the world, rows of classrooms lined along a corridor are being replaced by a number of varying-sized teaching spaces which open freely off usable multi-purpose passages. Spaces can be used by different-sized groups, or all can be used together as one large area for joint activities. This sort of planning cuts down on quantity, space and building material and gives flexibility and openness. Here, definitely, the reduction of quantity reduces costs and gives greater facilities for teaching and learning.

Quality, on the other hand, is not quite so easily dealt with for there are many of us who would rather have no building at all than reduce the quality of our building. However, the concept of quality means different things to different people. When we use the word in connection with our buildings it is invariably related to high-cost and/or a sophisticated finish. Little thought is given to the individual quality of the basic structural materials, the craftsmanship of those materials, or the 'surpassing merit' of the plan with its functional honesty. Such 'quality' is often only a deception, for underneath it is found poor brick or stone work with little skill of bonding, correct cornering, angles, joints, and little excellence is found in the mortar filling or vertical joints. In fact the work generally shows that the craftsmen are conscious that within a few days their work will be covered with plaster and, so, often they consider that good quality of work is a mere waste.

In such a system we need to review our sense of values. I would argue that an improvement in quality, as opposed to the apparent 'quality finish' is cost-reducing and it is an improvement to building, not a deterioration. It is a setting up of standards.

Our buildings have many architectural gimmicks which are mainly functionless. When one person covers his façade with flooring tiles, in a month twenty other buildings start slapping on flooring tiles. One man puts in two large round circular holes in functionless walls, and in no time the whole city produces round holes in functionless walls. One man paints his pebble-dashed front with tasteful shades of that entrancing colour Sunkist Dung Superdupercem with the offsets picked out in Drongo Blue-Black—and the next week every corner of the town glows with Sunkist Dung picked out with Drongo Blue-Black. We all are well aware of the cost of these fancy finishes.

Our checker-board planning and use of land is extravagant of roads, water and electricity supply services and of sanitation and drainage. Similarly, we scatter our plumbing, sanitation and electricity all over the building plans whereas a bit of streamlining would bring all these services together into a single core. Elaborate RC frames which use a lot of short-supply materials like cement and steel are often extremely elaborate and cumbersome not only to carry walls which could just as easily have been themselves the load-bearing element, but also to provide all these gimmicks of pointless, beam-end projections, our much-loved cantilevers and protrusions, and our vastly elaborate sun shades (when a sensible roofing system would have done the same job more simply and effectively). In these spheres streamlining would bring about great cost-reductions.

Quantity will definitely affect costs, while streamlining of planning, services, structural systems, building techniques and finishes can all be done by increasing true quality with certain cost-reduction effects. I find that most cost-reduction techniques give better quality and give our architecture an Indian identity that supercedes the imitation cosmopolitan modern stuff with which we are defacing our cities today.

Paper presented at a symposium on 'Building Cost Reduction' (sponsored by the Department of Technical Education, 22 March 1975)

We Need a Programme

In the summer 1978 issue of *Shelter*, J.B. D'Souza, the country's Secretary to the Ministry of Works and Housing, wrote:

> We need a programme:
> 1. That uses up very little of the usual building materials which are so scarce, and adopts local materials instead;
> 2. That draws on a reserve of private entrepreneurship which has not yet been seriously tapped;
> 3. And that cost very little.

During my thirty years of professional activity in India I have been increasingly fascinated by the subject of the use of building materials. Naturally, as an architect, I tend to divide the population into two groups—those engaged in the building industry, and others. I have come to the conclusion (quite a long time ago) that it is we professionals who are conservative and stick-in-the-mud and often I am tempted to add the description 'obstructionist'. The layman, on the other hand, I find innovative, ingenious and full of an amazing faith.

D'Souza's first point relates to the use of materials for house building. Leaving aside materials used for electrical and sanitation works, you can almost count the list of materials used by architects, engineers and building contractors on the fingers of one hand: burnt bricks and tiles, cement and sand, steel, timber and glass. As we've started counting on to the second hand you can add stone, which they use sparingly and mainly as a substitute for aggregate in concrete, and there are sheet materials of galvanized iron and asbestos cement. Finally there are the fancy finishes, paints, and alternative metal for 'iron-mongery' and frames like aluminium. These few materials are used by housing professionals all over the country and the resulting so-called 'modern house' looks much the same, regardless of climate or location. As D'Souza implies, most of these items are becoming scarce and increasingly costly.

Furthermore, because we are all demanding the same materials wherever we build the two big bottlenecks of transport and fuel get tighter and more restrictive each year.

Now let us take a look at the approach to the use of materials for building by *the others*—that is the 'ordinary man', 'the layman', 'the people', the 'amateur', the 'do-it-yourself-because-its-the-only-way-to-get-anything-done man'. He starts off by using materials used by the professional when he can afford it. If he thinks he can use bricks, he makes use of a wide range of sizes and does not insist on oddities, such as a 'metric brick', and makes use of whatever is locally available. Some bricks are thin, some thick, some are large and block-like, others are a little more than tiles; some are solid, others are hollow; some are yellow, some red, some grey or black and others almost white, but they all get used. He uses tiles for floors, roofs and cladding. He uses the 'proper' Mangalore tile, but I have collected nearly twenty other varieties of ingenious interlocking tile. He uses the flat 'English' or 'Company' or 'Fish' tile and he has a very large range of so-called 'country' tile. (I have seen nearly thirty variations of this tile.) But we professionals stick grimly to the Mangalore tile, that is if we remain sufficiently old-fashioned as to want to use tile at all. Most people do not realize that there are several times more country-tile roofs in India than there are 'proper' Mangalore tile or RC or sheet roofs. If the country tile is used so widely, with all its defects and shortcomings, why have we not improvized on it and why do we not use it? (By 'we' I mean, 'we professionals'.)

Stone is extensively used by the 'ordinary man' wherever he finds it—and while the professionals only know about squared and random rubble (they love to cover modern buildings with sheets of thin marble which seem to come alarmingly unstuck from time to time) the layman has many ways of making use of stone—of any degree of 'hardness' or shape, regular or irregular. Optimum use of stone is made by the layman for walls, floors and roofs. Stones used include slate-like stones which are easily split into thin sheets and a variety of ingeniously and decoratively made slabs of small irregular-shaped stones.

Wood has been used by both the layman and the professional, but now its forbidding cost prevents its general free use. Here the general approach of the professional is that only teak is good enough to use while the ordinary person has no hesitation in using the so-called 'country woods'. They are used for frames, doors, windows and *almaris*. He also uses split shingles of bark. A month ago I came across some beautiful purlins of bundles of five to ten millimetres thick twigs intricately bound together. The house I discovered using this system has been up for seventy years!

Now let us look at manufactured materials. Of these, cement heads the list. No professional, it seems, can ever think of building without a liberal usage of cement in many forms. If there is a shortage or a crisis, the work stops and the building schemes get shelved until the supply of cement is resumed. We all proclaim that cement is essential for concrete, mortar, plaster, flooring, sanitary works, surfacings, water-proofings, and so on. But ordinary people have many other alternatives. The commonest of these is lime but they also know a lot about the use of pozzolanas; or they use muds and clays very effectively in a variety of ways. Complete walls, in many areas, are often load-bearing and have lasted for over a hundred years; and in other situations and areas the same effective results are obtained by using mud and clay for mortars and plasters. In several regions of the country dry stone walls are a real work of art and the most durable. I have used this dry stone-walling technique for my own house when I first settled in Kerala. I was charged, by the local craftsman, nine rupees for a hundred cubic of walling which included the cost of collecting the rocks off the site, breaking and building them. Even now it would cost a little less than twice that.

Those who know me are aware that sooner or later the subject of mud comes into all my conversation. I have already let it creep into the previous paragraph on cement and I can't stop myself from reminding you that we professionals won't even look at the idea of using mud, let alone get down to specifying and using it. But just think of the position mud holds in the overall housing pattern throughout the country. No other material is used so extensively. As I write this, within a few hundred yards of me are many houses of nothing but mud, carrying substantial timber frames and tile or thatch roofs, and which are over a hundred years old. A variety of soils can be used. If the soil by itself is not satisfactory, there are many additives used to remedy the fault or

259

shortcoming of the local earth. 'Secret' techniques handed down and developed through generations are almost as numerous as districts in the land. Mud is used by itself. It is often load-bearing, and is sometimes reinforced with a wide variety of materials, besides being stabilized with another range of local products. It is used as a daub or plaster. Like pastry, it can be plain or fancy. It is used as a binder, mortar, plaster or as decoration. But none of this is even considered for use by the professional. The poor layman uses little else.

Next we come to the non-professional flair for using agricultural and forest by-products and waste. Oh, the number of seminars I've been to be told about this wonderful idea of recycling wastes, etc. Nothing much seems to have resulted from all this expensive talk and not many of us seem to have noticed that roughly speaking, about seventy-five per cent of the buildings in India contain considerable quantities of these 'new wonder materials'—like bamboo, reeds, grasses, canes, barks, leaves, stalk or even roots. Similarly, there is considerable and ingenious use of industrial wastes—think of all the wayside teashops with their grills made from strips to punched-out metal-sheeting. And in slums one sees walls incorporating effectively the use of spring mattresses, motor-car radiators, cart wheels, tin cans, bottles, chains and a host of other industrial junk!

I think I've said enough. My point is that the professional displays little but caution and distrust; while the layman shows ingenuity, imagination, perseverance and a great and shining faith. I will unhesitatingly claim that far more research and development has been done by our ancestral laymen than by present-day scientists and professionals within the building industry. So what D'Souza is asking for is for nothing new or outlandish or impossible. It also establishes the fact that we do already have a talented flourishing 'private entrepreneurship'. As for cost, whenever I spend hours struggling over the cost of my so-called 'low-cost' house, I go and look at the local people putting up houses for themselves, with perhaps the occasional help of a mason or a carpenter, and it shames and thrills me to find them talking of the final cost of houses in figures of hundreds and not thousands.

This perhaps indicates that we, building and housing professionals and 'experts', are not the right people to be tackling the vast housing problems and needs of the country today. I am convinced that with the present current ideas and systems we cannot give D'Souza the programme the country expects him to produce. I think if we are willing to eat the humble pie and seek and follow the guidance of the traditional housing experts, that is the ordinary man who has to build for himself, we may be able to go much further with this vast task of housing the homeless while we and they are still alive.

(unpublished)

Roofs for Roofless Millions

Swaminathan S. Aiyar's very fine article on our 'Roofless Millions' is most timely and we all need to be reminded time and time again of the terrible state of affairs concerning the huge number of Indian families without any form of shelter and millions more with not only whole families, but often two and three families all living together in only one room. Even these 'rooms' are concocted from a collection of opened-up tin cans, semi-water-proofed sacks, broken bits of old asbestos cement sheeting, and the walls are made of bits of sticks and old rags and bags. None of us should be able to sleep easily with two-thirds of our urban population living under such conditions. Add to this horrible picture the nasty details of the almost complete lack of sanitation of any sort and the fact that a window is almost unknown, and we should be thoroughly ashamed of ourselves.

Aiyar is lavish with facts and figures and his assessment of the situation is down-to-earth and realistic. His point is also well taken that there is no going back from this flow of population from the villages to the cities. It is unfortunate and sad that the biggest flow is to the few, really overcrowded, large cities. This is merely because there is a similar flow of business and industry in the same direction. To build up facilities and amenities of the larger towns and smaller cities so that industry would spread more evenly across the country was the hoped-for policy of both Jawaharlal Nehru and Indira Gandhi, but industries still sprout like mushrooms around the four main cities of the country. So the town-planning nightmares enlarged upon by Aiyar are more or less inevitable and, as he also points out clearly and rightly, we have to accept the facts of life and plan for the best we can do for the apparently inevitable urban jungle.

The urban housing shortage (dwelling units) are about 5.2 million with a five-yearly increase of over two million, and to meet these housing needs in the next ten years we will spend about 44,000 crores of rupees. (Perhaps this figure makes a little more impact if we write it down in full—Rs 44,000,00,00,000!) I want to add to these horrific figures by reminding us that the rural population is three times greater than the urban one. The fact that there is a steady migration of rural people to the cities does not mean that they leave behind them lakhs of empty 'desirable residences'! Numerically, if not spectacularly, we have more rural slums than urban ones. To the starry-eyed, rural slums may have a more romantic air about them because of cows, goats, hens and banyan trees—but the services are considerably less and the rate of increase of population is greater.

These figures clearly show that the task of coping with this enormous need for housing is not a little side issue to the other and main work of the Public Works Department(PWD). I believe that the very fact that we can even contemplate spending a figure like Rs 44,000 crores, should mean that we need an establishment whose sole aim is to cope with this vast task of giving the economically weaker section of seven million families houses, however small, to live in during the coming Five Year Plan period. Our PWDs have a-hundred-and-one-tasks to cope with— dams, docks, bridges, roads, public buildings of all sorts, all requiring engineering skills. Almost all our housing boards show a marked preference for building for the high- and middle-income groups. They also prefer to hand over loans and grants for others to deal with the actual construction work of putting up low income group and EWS housing. Furthermore, they are autonomous bodies whose board members are mainly political nominees who decide on their own policies of what they will build and for whom they will build and at what cost they will build.

Is it not high time, therefore, that a body is created with nothing, absolutely nothing but this one single goal of providing seven million basic houses in the next five years?

What would be the shape of such a body with a chance of accomplishing even half of the seven million goal? Don't forget that very very few housing boards or other institutions or departments dealing with housing manage to put up LIG and EWS houses in thousands a year, let alone lakhs. The typical housing board staff is dominated by a very large group of highly-trained and qualified engineers, aided by a few architects and a few administrators and clerical staff who are at their diposal. Whenever I am designing or building small 200 square feet houses costing Rs 4,000–5,000 each, I always wonder where these excellent, experienced, highly and expensively trained engineers and architects fit into the picture.

Engineers are not a necessary part of the permanent staff of the body we need actually to construct a few million houses. The same goes for architects. We are not going to require seven million individual plans and designs! At the most there will be fifty (more likely it will boil down to five) variations of one or two basic plans to cope with varying regional and climatic requirements. Town-planners. Yes, *if* they will promise to always keep in mind this one simple single goal of seven million EWS houses all over the country in accessible places and on very limited land.

What we will need most are down-to-earth (rather literally in this case) top quality adminstrators of the civil service type. They will have to see to the location and acquisition and distribution of land. They will have to organize the continuous availability, in very large quantities, of simple local building materials and local transport to get them to the building sites. They will have the organizing of workshops for producing a large and steady flow of the simplest doors and windows, etc. They have to organize the daily availability of cash to pay for labour and materials on the spot. All this contracting nonsense and only-being-paid-when-work-has-been-done-to-a-certain-level will not work when we are to involve ordinary people and labourers and craftsmen in a tremendous labour-intensive job.

These tasks must be seen as simple, direct, straightforward ones. Nothing complex must be allowed to creep in. This is a vast industry with very very few ingredients and only one simple goal. Quick decisive administration and organization is what is called for in a big way. It must be seen as a small, efficient, well-oiled hub in the middle of a large wheel rim that has to revolve steadily, without ceasing, seven million revolutions. For the seven million families awaiting a proper, however small, roof over their heads it will really be a revolution! Certainly up till now none of our many existing building construction bodies has shown itself capable of producing one-thousandth of what we are hoping for.

There are apprehensions expressed about our Five Year plans—and it is all too easy to be critical—but it does seem to be true that much of the planning is in the form of an effort to improve on the performance of the previous plan programmes. Housing has always had a prominent part in all these plans, but we always fall far short of our targets. All the plan housing proposals expect the programmes to be achieved through the existing machinery and establishments, and if one thing is clear it is that all these agencies achieve a pitifully small proportion of what is hoped for.

Let us therefore leave the PWD type of establishments to deal with the many genuine engineering needs of the country (and there is certainly no dearth of such needs and no question of 'chopping' engineers!). But let us plan realistically for this one simple, single goal of say five million houses in the next five years, and let us use only such people who are absolutely necessary for the carrying out of such a plan.

No one these days even attempts to refute the allegations that an enormous amount of building money is siphoned off into ever increasing number of pockets. Whole establishment systems are now attuned and geared to this siphonage and all seem to accept it as inevitable. If we attempt this EWS housing plan by 'the direct method' we have a chance to show that siphonage is not an essential ingredient of India's management system.

I don't want to challenge some of Aiyar's ideas about what these five million homes are going to look like! His facts and figures make me shudder in concern and shame. His dreams of 'high and straight' buildings make me shudder in horror! Nature only goes in for proportionate height and very rarely for 'straight'. One of the areas where we waste an enormous amount of building money is in fighting nature, when we should be conserving money and materials and energy by going along with it. However, the designing of seven million houses should be no problem to India's architects and there is no reason why small should be ugly. The bigger problem is how to get these seven million houses up before 1990.

Indian Express
December 1984

Proposal for a Core House

While travelling in rural India one realizes that an enormous number of people have made their own 'shelters'. We tend to call them 'huts' 'hovels', not 'houses'—they have the basic protection of some walls and a roof, but little else. There is often no water supply or sanitation, and cooking is done outside. It is not that these amenities are not required, but just that a fair amount of money has to be spent on them. Mud and thatch, on the other hand, merely require a bit of skill and manual labour.

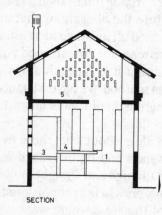

SECTION

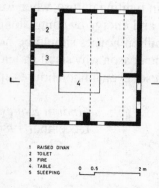

1 RAISED DIVAN
2 TOILET
3 FIRE
4 TABLE
5 SLEEPING

0 0.5 2 m

If and when the government or other agencies want to build for such families, it would be far more sensible to provide essentials like a water supply and a latrine, rather than a structure which they can normally build themselves.

Obviously with time factor, weather, seasonal occupation and so on we cannot just dump these facilities on an empty site and tell the occupant to build a house round them. So we should provide the absolute minimum of a house—a minimum that will include the essentials of fire, water and waste disposal.

I think it is better to build a small tower, so that the minimum building is high enough to accommodate a built-in sleeping platform and a work table at the ground level, and a naturally-vented loft space. A small segregated cooking area and a separate toilet can also be part of the

266

same core volume. Later, if and when funds are available, people should be able to acquire other 'building units' when their occupations give them the opportunity for constructing their own walls, doors, windows, roofs, etc. They can also build a perimeter wall with other facilities attached, with lean-to roofs, sheds, stores, animal and work areas, covered spaces within their own secure bit of land.

(unpublished)

APPENDICES

Appendix 1

Introduction to Laurie Baker's Drawings and Sketches

The designing and making of a building is the result of numerous influences and assimilations, but the nature of these influences can be gauged only by the way they are perceived and recorded by the architect. The research and survey of a place and its people for projects, has held an endless fascination for Baker. The settings for living created by him and the desire for personalized detail comes from the architect's own compulsion to make a meticulous documentation of the places he visits and inhabits.

Baker keeps a diligently prepared notebook on the hospital he has visited, the village he has designed in, and also the ordinary people he meets every day. His comments on institutions of the government (the roads of Kerala) and on cultural and private idiosyncrasies (the tying of the *mundu*), suggest an artistic ability to record a place with objective faultlessness, as well as offer subjective home truths.

Baker's perception of design and his interpretation of life are illustrated here in his documentation of two places which he had visited: the first is a set of sketches of a church in Goa; and the second is a documentation of a village in Andhra Pradesh for which he was asked professional help on developing designs for cyclone shelters.

Details of a Church in Goa

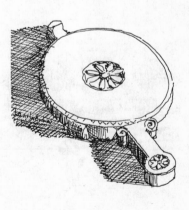

273

Details of Ramapuram (Kuppam) in Andhra

view west to next village: away from the lake and looking towards the distant hills

fishing village, 55 kms north of Madras—fishing in the Pulikat lake

274

a fisherman's house

Small conical mud and thatch houses.

Floors: either beaten mud leeped with thin cow-dung, or mud and lime plaster beaten very smooth and shiney.

Walls: no foundations. Walls of mud, nothing extra added. The men do the work. 3 ft. to 4–6 ft. high.

Supports (for small veranda): mainly rough straight timber about 3–4 ft. high and 4–5 in. diameter.

Roof frame: rafters rough, of bamboo, split palm trunks, or rough timber, max. size about 3 in. x 2 in., often much smaller. These are tied onto hoops of cane to form a cone which sits on the mud wall. (Sometimes small wooden 'anchors' are bedded in the mud.)

no *Windows*

Doors: mainly 3 planks (each 5 ft. 6 in. × 1 ft. × 1 in.) nailed with big iron spikes on to 3 battens (horizontal wooden frame of about 3 in. x 4 in. timber).

Roofing: coconut or palmyra leaves tied on the rafters — then rice straw thatch on top — all held down with an inch thick rice straw ropes.

most *Plans:* are circular. Very few roughly square. One or two, only, rectangular.

the out-of-doors cooking place in the open yard

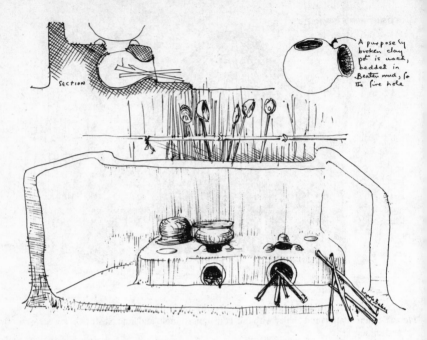

SECTION

A purposely broken clay pot is used, bedded in beaten mud, for the fire hole

drawing water from wells

Appendix 2

Laurie Baker's Cost-Reduction Manual

In 1972, Achuta Menon, the then Chief Minister of Kerala, realized the potential of Baker's work. And so he sought to use Baker's ideas for streamlining the numerous housing programmes of the state. These were incorporated in a handy guide for laymen in a simple step-by-step fashion. The manual was published by the Centre of Science and Technology for Rural Development (COSTFORD).

As Menon said about the manual, 'I wanted it written so that even I, as a Minister, would be able to understand it. It was meant to be a manual for Kerala, translated into Malayalam and provided to every local building office and district headquarters.'

Virtually all practical samples of building and cost-reduction that were found in similar manuals by other government organizations had already been demonstrated in Baker's work—so putting it together was simple. A garbled, cliché-ridden copy had been prepared by engineers of the Public Works Department (PWD), which was later re-worded by Baker into a simple text with line illustrations.

Copies of the manual, published in English and Malayalam, were sent to district collectors, tehsildars and panchayats. 'Occasionally,' says Baker, 'a good man will be transferred out to some remote tribal area—as all good men often are—there he'll produce the book and say "I want a core house built just as in the book?" But such instances are rare....'

The manual gives a logical analysis of how the design, production and assembly of different components of a building—walls, foundations, roofs and windows—can be simplified, and, in the wasteful, budget-conscious programmes of government housing, made more cost-conscious. Even today, nearly twenty years after its publication, this humble work carries a range of common-sense ideas that are equally relevant today.

Some excerpts from the manual are given in this appendix.

Houses: How to Reduce Building Costs

Building houses is a costly business these days. A lot of the current expenditure is on unnecessary fashionable frills and designs. Much money could be saved merely by using common sense, along with simple, established, tried building practices. Every item that goes to make up a building has its cost. So always ask yourself the question: is it necessary? If the answer is 'no', then don't do it! The following pages attempt to show graphically the current and often expensive ways of doing things, compared with the simplest, less-expensive ways of building. The saving on each individual item may be small, but if you can cut down every rupee's worth of the current cost by twenty-five paise, a ten-thousand rupee house can be built for Rs 7,500. In saving and cutting down costs, the coice is *yours*. Do not allow the architect, the engineer, the building contractor to be dictators. You tell them what you want!

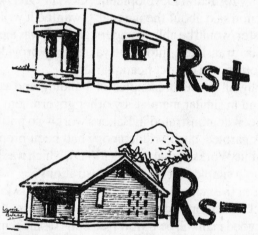

You often hear people describing houses as 'modern' or 'old-fashioned'. The so-called modern house is often merely fashionable but foolish, simply because it is expensive and does not take into account the locally-available inexpensive materials or the local climatic conditions or the actual needs of the occupants. Quite often the so-called 'old-fashioned' house demonstrates that the choice of building materials is important because it is less expensive and does not use up unnecessarily, materials that are in short supply and needed for other uses. It also copes effectively with weather hazards, such as strong sun, heavy rain, strong winds, high humidity, etc.

The two sketches typify the small 'modern house' at the top and an old-fashioned one below. The modern house is 'cubist' in design and uses a lot of cement plaster and paint. The roof does not protect the walls from rain and sun with the result that it is not very comfortable or convenient to live in. The 'old-fashioned' house has a sloping roof which quickly sheds heavy rain, protects walls from getting damp and from absorbing heat from the sun. Some of the windows have been replaced with *jalis*, which are cheaper and give permanent ventilation and light and protection or security.

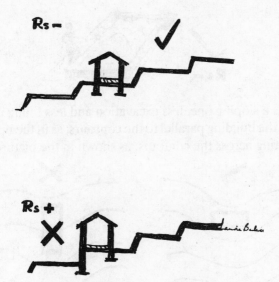

If you have to build your house on a terraced site, it is less expensive to place it in the middle of the terrace.

The lower picture shows the extra and more costly foundation and basement wall that has to be built if the building is near the edge of the terrace.

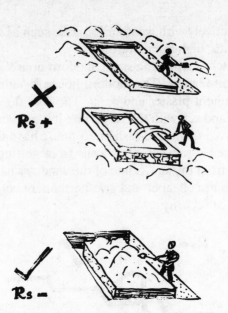

If the site is a sloping one, less excavation and less filling up is needed if you place the building parallel to the contours, as in the upper picture, and not cutting across the contours, as shown in the picture above.

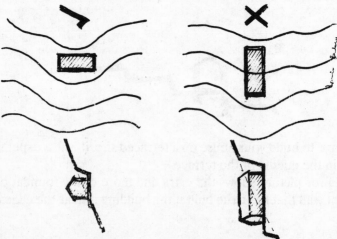

When excavating the trenches for the houses' foundations, labourers dig out the soil and throw it in all directions, especially outwards. After the basement walls have been completed they then shovel all the soil back again as infilling. If they shovel the soil inwards it will already be where it is wanted for infilling and some of the expense of excavation and infilling will have been saved.

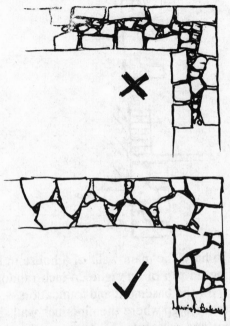

Masons are often more concerned with the outward appearance of a stone wall than with its strength and stability. The upper sketch shows a plan of a stone wall as it is usually built, with big, flat-faced stones on the outside while the middle of the wall is filled in with bits and pieces.

The lower plan shows how stones should be bonded, that is they dovetail in with stones on the other side of the wall and therefore give a much stronger and more durable wall. A properly bonded stone wall hardly needs mortar, and certainly a mud mortar is adequate, whereas the upper typical wall is not really safe without using a cement or lime mortar.

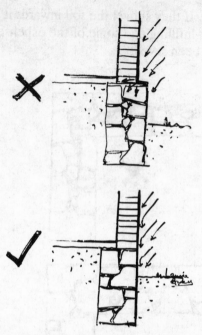

A common practice is to have the main walls of a house in nine-inch thick burnt bricks, sitting on top of an eighteen-inch random rubble (roughly-shaped stones) for the basement and foundation.

This means that there is a step where the nine-inch wall sits on the eighteen-inch wall below, and rain-water tends to seep in and weaken the lower stone wall, as shown in the upper picture.

For single and double storey houses it is better to put the outer side of nine-inch brick wall flush with the outer side of the eighteen-inch stone wall so that rain-water running down the wall does not soak into the wall.

This is also less costly because the eighteen-inch stone wall surrounding a room of a particular area (say 200 square feet) is larger (cubic content more) in the upper drawing.

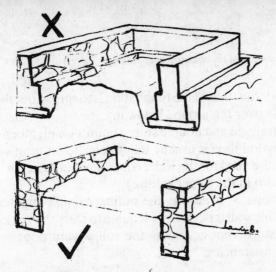

After building a house there is often little cash left over for furniture.
   Built-in seats, beds, work tables, etc. can easily and inexpensively be
had, merely by building the basement wall to a suitable height as shown
in the lower sketch.

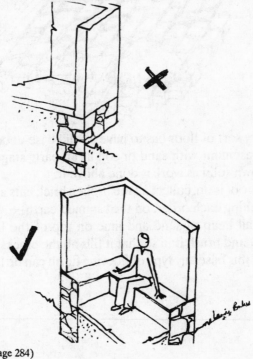

(see text on page 284)

(see illustration at the bottom of page 283)

The object or function of the foundation is to spread out the total weight of the house over the ground below it.

For small single and double storey houses on eighteen-inch (45 cm) wide foundation base is usually fully adequate on most soils and there is not often the need for the wider concrete layer beneath the basement wall (as shown in the upper picture).

Where stone is available, the ordinary simple eighteen-inch thick random rubble wall is perfectly adequate to carry the full load of a single or double storey house, unless the soil is very poor or loose or of different consistencies.

Almost every sort of floor has to have a solid base under it.

Fill the basement with sand or soil at an early stage and it will get trampled down solid as work is done above it.

After the roof is on, collect all the broken brick bats and lay them side by side, touching each other, on the rammed earth.

Mix a small heap of sand and lime on top of the bricks, and then spread it out and brush it in so that it fills all the cracks.

On top of this base any type of flooring finish can be laid successfully.

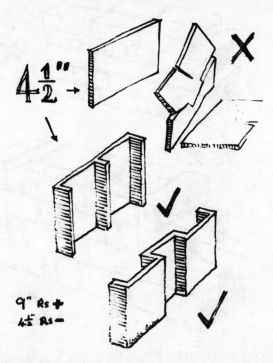

$4\frac{1}{2}'' \rightarrow$

$9''$ Rs +
$4\frac{1}{2}''$ Rs −

From a structural stability point of view, a four-and-a-half inch thick brick wall is often adequate for small single-storey houses, and certainly for interior partition walls. An isolated straight four-and-a-half inch thick wall is weak and can either fall over, or be knocked over, or can be crushed by the weight of the roof it carries. But it can be perfectly strong and capable of carrying the load of roofs and floors if it has either thin buttresses every five or six feet (as in the middle picture) or if recesses are created (as in the lower picture).

Similarly corners and intersecting walls are strengthening points in a thin wall.

These recesses can be used for shelves and *almirahs* at almost no extra cost!

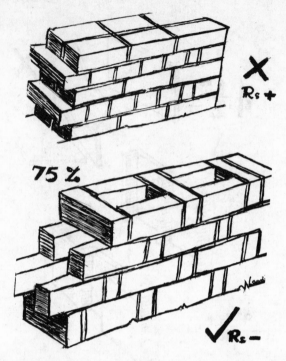

If burnt-brick is available, and if a nine-inch thick wall is required, then twenty-five per cent of the total number of bricks, and of the cost of the wall, can be saved by using a 'rat-trap' bond. It is simple to build, looks well, has better insulation properties and is as strong as the ordinary solid nine-inch thick brick wall.

The orthodox English bond is shown at the top, and the rat-trap bond below.

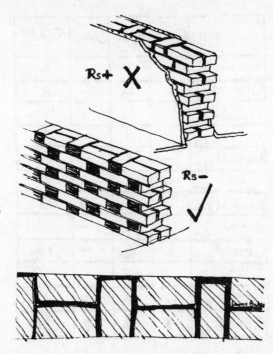

Bricks are often slightly irregular in length. So even if you can get a smooth 'fair face' on one side of a wall, the other side will be lumpy and irregular. Therefore, many builders say you must plaster the wall. But plaster is costly (it accounts for up to ten per cent of the total cost of a building). Also, there are the painting and maintenance costs of plaster to be considered.

The middle sketch and the lower plan show how the mortar can fill over the sunken end of the brick to produce a special fair face on the second side of the wall. Plaster is not required and a pleasing pattern has been made. Besides it has no painting and maintenance costs.

	Cement	Lime	Surki	Sand
Rich mix Rs+	1	—	—	6
General Rs-	1	—	—	8
For Stone Fdn & Basement Rs=	1	—	—	10
Rich mix Rs+	—	1	—	2
General Rs-	—	1	—	3
Rich mix Rs+	—	1	2	4
General Rs-	—	1	2	6
Rich mix Rs+	1	3	—	12
General Rs-	1	4	—	14
For Stone Fdn & Basement Rs=	1	5	—	16
Rich mix Rs+	1	2	4	18
General Rs-	1	2	4	20

This chart shows a variety of the mixes of cement, sand, lime and *surkhi* (finely-ground burnt clay) to give different plasters and mortars according to the function for which they are needed and according to the cost and availability of these several ingredients.

At present cement and sand only are commonly used. This is easy to mix and use, and it sets quickly. Lime and sand can give an equally strong mortar but it takes longer to set, and lime mortars have mainly gone 'out of fashion'. Similarly, good strong mortars are made by adding *surkhi* to lime and sand. These too are slow setting and 'unfashionable'. The slow setting problem can be solved by adding to the lime, or lime and *surkhi* mixes, a small amount of cement. All these variations are in this table.

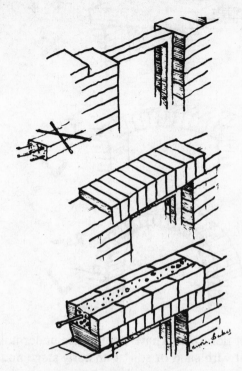

Lintels are usually made of reinforced concrete. Steel and cement are used.

Very often a lintel is not necessary over door and window openings up to four feet in width.

Ordinary brick-on-edge, as shown in the middle picture, is all that is required.

If something stronger is necessary, a hollow arrangement of bricks-on-edge, as in the lower picture, filled with one or two steel rods in concrete will carry very large weights of wall and roof etc. above.

This type of lintel is less than half the cost of the orthodox reinforced concrete lintel.

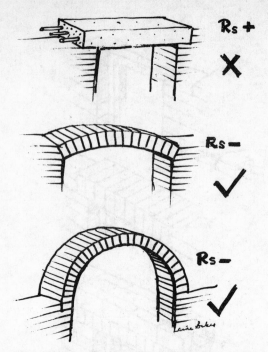

Almost every sort of floor has to have a solid base under it.

Fill the basement with sand or soil at an early stage and it will get trampled down solid as work is done above it.

After the roof is on, collect all the broken brick bats and lay them side by side, touching each other, on the rammed earth.

Mix a small heap of sand and lime on top of the bricks and then spread it out and brush it in so that it fills all the cracks.

On top of this base any type of flooring finish can be laid successfully.

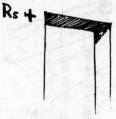

The most inexpensive way of spanning a hole in a wall is the simple 'corbel' arch. Each row of bricks projects two-and-a- quarter-inch beyond the course below until the bricks meet together in the middle. No formwork or shuttering is necessary.

This picture also demonstrates the fact that if you remove a door or a window, the whole wall will not fall down! Probably nothing will fall at all, but if it does, the maximum will be the amount of wall within the triangle above the frame. This triangle of bricks is, in fact, all that a lintel carries, and not the whole wall and half the roof above it.

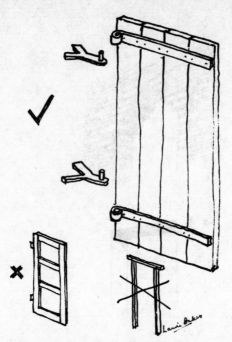

Door frames cost a lot of money and are often not actually necessary.

This picture shows how planks can be screwed together by strap iron hinges to form a door, and this carried by 'hold-fasts' built into the wall, thus eliminating the outer door frame altogether.

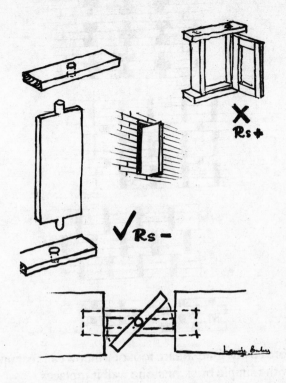

When a window is a necessity it is quite a costly item as shown in the top right hand corner.

The simplest window consists of a vertical plank set into two holes (or pivot hinges), one at the top and one at the bottom. The traditional design consists of two short wood pieces with a circular hole in each, and the vertical shutter has two small round protrusions (as shown on the left) to fit into the holes. Only a nine-inch wide hole is necessary for the 'window'.

This is strong, simple, inexpensive, requires very little labour, no iron mongery, lets in light and air and provides security.

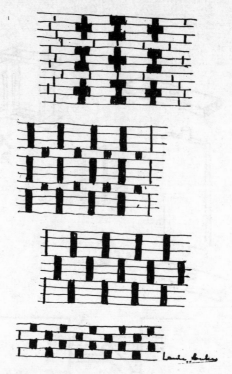

Windows are costly. One square foot of window can cost up to ten times the cost of the simple brick or stone wall it replaces.

A window has varied functions: to look out of, to let light inside a room, to let in fresh air, to let out stale air, and so on. In many of these situations a *jali* or 'honey-combed' wall is just as effective. Far from being a lot more costly than the basic wall, if made of brick it can be less costly than the house wall.

The bottom picture shows the simple honey-comb brick pattern. Wide vertical joints are left open and not filled with mortar.

The pictures above show a few of the many possible variations. This is an excellent inexpensive alternative to the costly window.

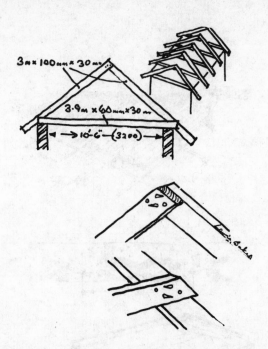

3m × 100mm × 30mm

3·9m × 60mm × 30mm

→ 10'-6" —(3200) ←

Anyone who can use a saw and a hammer can put together a simple, strong roof of timber over rooms up to twelve feet (3.65 m) wide. Three pieces of wood are nailed together and this simple 'trussed rafter' sits directly on top of any wall.

No wall plates and no ridge poles are necessary.

The traditional timber roofs are beautiful, but often quite elaborate and extravagant with the use of wood and call for a lot of skill.

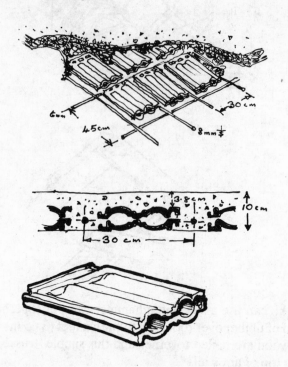

Timber is becoming too scarce and costly.

Galvanized iron and asbestos cement sheets use less timber, but iron rusts and is very hot to live under while those who work in asbestos factories and who live and work under AC roofs tend to develop lung cancer, so we should discourage its use and manufacture. Reinforced cement concrete slabs are very costly and use a lot of iron and cement.

As there is quite a lot of unnecessary concrete in an orthodox RCC slab we can replace some of this redundant concrete with any light-weight, cheap material in order to reduce the overall cost of the slab. This alternative RCC roof is called a filler slab. For fillers we can use light-weight bricks, or Mangalore or country tiles, or hourdies etc. This will reduce the cost of the orthodox RCC slab by about thirty or thirty-five per cent. As roofs and intermediate floors account for twenty to twenty-five per cent of the total cost of a house, the saving by using a filler slab is considerable.

The top picture shows how two waste Mangalore tiles come together to form an excellent light-weight filler, and how they are placed between the steel reinforcement rods creating a grid of RCC or beams. The lower picture shows a section through the slab.

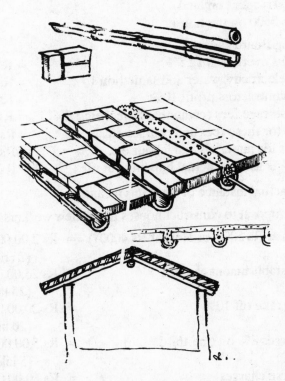

A good mature bamboo can also be split in half and used as a permanent shuttering for reinforced cement concrete ribs between brick units (three burnt bricks previously joined together with mortar to form a small slab).

This is a rural version of orthodox reinforced brick slab (RBC).

System of Establishment Charges in 1986

The following examples are percentages currently used by the Kerala State Housing Board.

Rs 8000 is spent on land and house for an Economically Weaker Section (EWS) family.
Approximately, of this sum:
    Rs 2500 is spent on land
    and Rs 5500 on the house.

The Housing Board charges	
for its overheads 12.5%	= Rs 690
for electricity, water and sanitation 15%	= Rs 725
for contractors profit 10%	= Rs 550
for storage fees (cement and steel etc.) 8%	= Rs 160
So the total for these fees and charges etc. is	Rs 2125
which leaves for materials and labour etc.	Rs 3375
So only 42% is used on actual building out of	Rs 8000

To take an actual instance of what this means:

There is a proposal to construct houses for cashew workers

4000 houses at Rs 5000(or 5000 at Rs 4000?)	= Rs 2,00,00,000
	(2 crores)
12.5% for establishment charges	= Rs 25,00,000
	(25 lakhs)
Contractors rake off 10%	= Rs 20,00,000
	(20 lakhs)
Storage charges 8% on one-third	= Rs 5,00,000
	(5 lakhs)
Total for these charges	= Rs 50,00,000
	(50 lakhs)

I consider a lavish arrangement for an 'Establishment' to deal with the building of these few thousand houses could be as follows:

1 Director say	Rs 25,000
10 Supervisors say	Rs 120,000
1 Architect say	Rs 10,000

Office expenses say	Rs 10,000(!)
Travel say	Rs 15,000
etc. say	Rs 20,000
Total	Rs 2,00,000

but the Housing Board would get Rs 50,00,000 for designing one small house.

Now consider the needs of the country. Let us say there will be a million houses put up all over the country during 1976.

This will cost (at the Rs 8000 per house figure)	800 crores
Of this land will cost	200 crores
and buildings will cost	600 crores

The establishment charges for the average State Housing Boards would be 12.5% (the highest allowed by the Act) + 75 crores.
This for designing one small house plan with, say, ten different variations to suit differing conditions throughout the land.

Contractors profits @ 10% come to	Rs 60 crores
and 'storage charges' to	Rs 16 crores
So charges alone account for	151 crores!

Suggest an 'Establishment' to deal with a country-wide million houses scheme in a year (half-a-lakh per state approximately)

1. Chairperson/Director	Rs 50,000
2. A committee of experts, say 20, to meet 5 times, at Rs 5,000 per member per time	Rs 5,00,000
3. 100 administrators or engineers or organisers at Rs 25000 each	Rs 25,00,000
4. 1000 juniors as supervisor-cum-work-organizer-and-buyer each at Rs 1000	Rs 1,20,00,000
5. Office rents	Rs 9,50,000
6. Printing and office work etc.	Rs 15,00,000
7. Travel etc.	Rs 18,00,000
Total	Rs 2,00,00,000
	(2 crores)

| Multiply by 10 for the benefit of sceptics | Rs 20 crores |
| But Housing Boards would have taken | Rs 151 crores! |

To me this clearly indicates that such 'low-cost schemes' should be separated and dealt with by their own small 'Establishment'.

Appendix 3

A Letter to the Minister for Works and Housing

Laurie Baker
The Hamlet
Nalanchira
Trivandrum

To the Minister for
Works and Housing
Kerala State Government

10 April 1984

Dear Sir,

I do hope you will pardon my writing to you like this but I feel more and more uncomfortable about our government's approach to the housing needs of the state, not to mention our construction output.

You are of course aware that I am not an Indian citizen but I have made India my home for the past nearly forty years and throughout that time I have been building with and for ordinary people, with whom I totally associate myself. As your Housing Commissioner often reminds me, I do not understand the way our government departments work (and I am sure I am not the only person worthy of such an assertion). But I have been quite closely associated and involved with such bodies as HUDCO, CBRI, UPDESCO, NID and the Planning Commission and Planning Board groups etc. so I feel I have these as a mild excuse for writing to you with a little bit of understanding of the housing needs of us all.

I put it that way because almost everyone with whom I talk about housing express their feelings that we, the government housing organizations do not apparently understand the actual housing needs of

301

ordinary people, and even if there is any understanding there seems to be precious little being done actually to meet those needs.

I have to make it very very clear that when I use the words 'ordinary people' I do not mean myself and the friends I have from the same social stratum. Taking census data, this 'ordinary' or 'average' person is rural, is not permanently employed, has next to no savings, and does not use a bank.

This letter is to plead with you to try and help change the attitudes, policies and performance of the Kerala State Housing Board (KSHB). I sincerely hope that you read through carefully the two letters about the Housing Board in today's *Express* page 3, because they are very very typical of how people see the Housing Board. The figures they quote are correct. This does mean that this sort of Housing Board Construction is costing Rs 400 per sq. ft. It does mean that the Housing Board thinks that a Middle Income Group (MIG) man can put down an advance payment of Rs 1.16 lakhs and can pay instalments of Rs 4,600 and pay 15 per cent interest too.

Instead of listening to these very valid criticisms by the people of Kerala, the Board tries only to justify itself and belligerently declares it is quite justified in building for the rich. To make this really clear its three senior officers go gadding off to the Gulf to see what they can do for all those poor Keralites who are slaving away in order to send us some foreign exchange—if the KSHB does not do something for them, everyone else will get houses and when they return they will have nothing. Our hearts really bleed for them.

Meanwhile the Board puts out its figures of building for the poor. There is your Voluntary Agencies Scheme. From time to time announcements about it are made in the press, but the fact remains that the lay people involved (i.e., these Voluntary Agencies) have no organization or personnel who know how to build large numbers of houses and they are all left with the problem of how to get the houses actually constructed. I know this to be a fact because they come to me asking me to build the houses for them.

Then there is the continual criticism by all that the KSHB is only concerned with High Income Group (HIG) and MIG housing. Again the Board tries to say that this is not true and that it has built for Economically Weaker Section (EWS) and Low Income Group (LIG).

But again, the actual fact is that the numbers of houses actually built by the Board are very few for both rich and poor—the actual figures of houses actually constructed by the KSHB in the past few years were: 1979–80, 525 houses, in 1980–91, 440 houses, in 1981–82, 404 houses, and in 1982–83, 165 houses; and of these four years production of a total of 1,567 houses, only 165 of them were for EWS. Of course, I am instantly jumped on when I quote these numbers and am told the Board has given so many sites and so many loans. But, Sir, I am concerned with actual numbers of houses produced and being lived in. You don't live on a vacant site and you do not live under a loan. I personally think that these figures, considering the number of highly qualified staff and considering a weekly wages bill of seven lakhs, and considering the clamourings of the people for tens if not hundreds of thousands of houses, are nothing but disgraceful. You should know that it is the considered opinion of a very large number of seriously thinking people that at present there is very very little to justify the continued existence of the Housing Board.

Another point to look at seriously is the fact that you organized the housing competition and the Board showed that it could build for Rs 6,000, but it now refuses to get down to it and build half-a-lakh or so, and instead it has just put up EWS houses costing well over twenty thousand rupees and sanctimoniously advises the Voluntary Agencies to get on with their building schemes and the Housing Board will give them plans and technical advice!!! Very hearty laughter, if it were not so pathetic.

If we are to build the houses the people of the state need, we have to go about it in a very different manner from what is currently being done, or not being done, as the case may be. It is agreed by most that to every one HIG house needed, there are three MIG houses needed and well over thirty LIG and EWS houses. It is generally now agreed that if we (including your Housing Commissioner) are to meet the housing needs of the state by the end of this century we need to build nearly one lakh of houses every year. Quite a lot—perhaps half(?)—may get built by ordinary people themselves—but the other half—probably about 45,000 EWS and LIG a year—will have to be put up by some government organization each year. So far, no government agency and no voluntary agency has shown itself capable of dealing with such numbers.

But it is very clear that there is a real and crying need for some such agency which is staffed only by personnel trained and fit and willing to build very simply and systematically, Engineers and Architects are not required, nothing either of them can do is built for four, five or six thousand rupees. You need a first class senior IAS man to head the organization and he should have powers and staff to acquire land, amass local building materials where needed (this means mud, laterite, granite, lime, etc.—not cement, steel or glass). He needs surveyors to lay out and mark out, he needs masons trained in cost-reducing methods to train as they build with other local masons, and he needs acccountants to have daily money available for daily work and material purchase etc.

However—it is not the purpose of this letter to suggest schemes and details. It is to say plainly and emphatically that the house building situation is very bad. Government costs are ridiculously high while ordinary people can build for twelve per cent of government costs. The wealthy, the HIGs, the Gulfers and the Singaporians etc. should look after themselves for five or ten years and the government agencies created to produce the needed houses for the state should get down to the actual job of building—constructing, putting up actual houses (and not get others to do it for them) especially for the poor. For this coming five to ten years, let the government only build for LIG and EWS families. If they can't or won't do it they should be disbanded and an organization created that will do it.

Again, I apologize for blowing my top at you, of all people, but I do have a respect for your understanding of 'ordinary people' I also want you to know that I am going to follow through this my 'personal campaign' about this housing situation wherever I feel anything constructive can result we have already discussed these matters at considerable length at Planning Commission meetings in Delhi and with our own Planning Board here, but what is most essential is a change of heart of our own Housing Board. I believe very much that you could guide them to a more realistic policy.

All very good wishes to you.

Yours sincerely,

(LAURIE BAKER)

Notes and References

1. Gautam Bhatia, 'Laurie Baker—Architect for the Common Man', interview in VISTARA, a Festival of India publication, New Delhi, 1986.
2. Laurie Baker, 'Low-Cost Buildings for All', *Hindustan Times*, New Delhi, 17 January 1974.
3. Laurie Baker, 'The Question of Taking Appropriate Building Technology to Pithoragarh', *Science and Rural Development in Mountains*, J.S. Singh, S.P. Singh and C. Shastri(eds.), Gyanodaya Prakashan, Naini Tal, 1980.
4. ibid.
5. ibid.
6. Laurie Baker, 'Low-Cost Buildings for All', op. cit.
7. Laurie Baker, 'Is a Modern Indian Architecture Possible?', *Spazio Societa*, Milan, 1986.
8. Laurie Baker, 'The Housing Situation in the Light of Social Attitudes', *Sciencereel*, Trivandrum University, Trivandrum, 1975.
9. Laurie Baker, 'Low-Cost Buildings for All', op. cit.
10. Laurie Baker, 'Is a Modern Indian Architecture Possible?', op. cit.
11. Laurie Baker, 'Does Building Cost-Reduction Mean Sacrifice of Quality?', paper presented at a symposium on 'Cost-Reduction Techniques in Building Construction', sponsored by GECSTA and the Department of Technical Education, March 1975.
12. Gautam Bhatia, 'Laurie Baker—Architect for the Common Man', op. cit.
13. Laurie Baker, 'The Housing Situation in the Light of Social Attitudes', op. cit.
14. Laurie Baker, 'Cementlessness', *Hindustan Times*, New Delhi, 4 November 1974.

15. Laurie Baker, 'Low-Cost Buildings for All', op. cit.

16. Gautam Bhatia, 'Laurie Baker—Architect for the Common Man', op. cit.

17. Gautam Bhatia, 'Baker in Kerala', *The Architectural Review*, August 1987.

18. Laurie Baker, 'Roofs for Roofless Millions', *Indian Express*, December 1984.

19. Gautam Bhatia, 'Laurie Baker—Architect for the Common Man', op. cit.

Other References

Gautam Bhatia, 'Architecture and Tradition', *World Architecture*, no. 7, London, 1990.

Gautam Bhatia, 'Architecture: Creating a Vernacular Idiom', *Indian Express*, 4 August 1985.

Gautam Bhatia, 'Home, Affordable Home', *Times of India*, 23 July 1989.

Gautam Bhatia, 'The Architecture of Laurie Baker', *Inside Outside*, Bombay, November–December 1989.

K.C. John, 'Laurie Baker's Houses for the Million', *Illustrated Weekly of India*, Bombay, 24 January 1982.

K. Govindan Kutty, 'Baker's Call for Keralavatkaranam', *Indian Express*, 30 November 1987.

Laurie Baker, 'Architectural Anarchy', *The India Magazine*, August 1984.

Laurie Baker, 'A Spoilt Child's Toy Blocks', *Indian Express*, 21 March 1983.

Laurie Baker, 'Houses: How to Reduce Building Costs', Centre of Science and Technology for Rural Development (COSTFORD), July 1986.

Laurie Baker, 'The Industrial Designer and Housing', paper presented at the seminar on 'Design for Development', at the National Institute for Design, Ahmedabad, 1979.

Laurie Baker, 'We Need a Program', paper presented at the HUDCO Conference, *Shelter*, Summer, 1978.

Pervin Mahoney, 'The Only Architect in India', *Inside Outside*, Bombay, December–January 1980.

P.G. Verughese, 'A Questing Conscience: the Life and Mission of a Radical Sage', *Architecture + Design*.

Robin Spence, 'The Wealth of Poor Resources', *Spazio Societa*, Milan, September–December 1981.

Index

309

Vikramapuram hill 98

walls
  of half-brick thickness 43, 109,
    189, 208
wash-basin 252
'witches-cap' roof 58

wood-and-thatch roof 78
wood lattice work 3
Women's hostel, Centre for
  Development Studies 169–170
Works and Housing Department
  231

$$45 \times 10 = 450$$
$$61 \times 5 = 305$$
$$\overline{755}$$